Uniquely Yucatan

This group of writings keenly reflects the encounters and cultural shocks of a new place of residence, full of light, sun, and warmth, both physical and human. With a friendly and precise style in each story, we find wisdom, humor, irony and good will. It is a book which gives out a friendly atmosphere, full of dialogue and emotional experiences. It's a bridge between languages and cultures constructed by a community which is enthusiastic and altruistic toward Yucatan.
Jorge Cortes Ancona ~ Chief, Department of Literature and Editors of the Secretariat of Culture and the Arts in Yucatan, Mexico.

A lively, generous, rewarding collection that will not only encourage readers to read, but to write as well.
John MacLachlan Gray ~ Canadian, novelist, essayist, writer-composer, television writer, and playwright (*Billy Bishop Goes to War*).

The occasionally touching, frequently amusing, often informative, ***Uniquely Yucatan***, a collection of the experiences of six women coping with and enjoying life in a foreign land, is a delightful read! Through poems and anecdotes–lots of language bloopers–the reader gains a kaleidoscopic understanding of why many visit the Yucatan and return to live. A wise person advised, "for you, from north of the Rio Bravo, time is money. For us in Yucatan, time is for living." Read these stories you will understand.

Uniquely Yucatan should grace every guesthouse bedside, and be given by realtors seeking to entice clients to make The Yucatan their home. Poet and mother of triplets, psychologist, Vancouver-Toronto-Broadway-London theater company manager, Cuban-American, nature photographer, and diplomat, who served, retired and returned; all are captivating storytellers, creating the kaleidoscope!
Grant Spradling ~ Author of *Maya Sacrifice* and three other novels.

I am very happy to write some of my impressions about this book. I appreciate the warm invitation. It's a great privilege to have in Merida, living among us, a group of United States and Canadian ladies who feel passion for writing poetry, stories, chronicles and articles about their experiences in Merida and in Yucatan. I know several of you and I also know your writing, which I have truly enjoyed. I've just finished reading *Speaking Spanish Like a Gringo, Sallie's Gift, La Peregrina, To Xocen, He Lives with Me, What I Meant To Say,* and others of the same quality, all based on the experiences of their authors in Yucatan, and I find in them sentimentality, tears and laughs, language problems, touches of humor and irony, and sincere commentaries. I enjoy the style of Maryetta, Lorna Gail, Theresa, Rainie, Gwen and the talented ornithologist and dear friend Cherie. Continue, dear colleagues, you have much to tell. And let me congratulate you.

Roldan Peniche Barrera - President of the Council for Editors of the Secretariat of Culture and the Arts in Yucatan, Mexico. Born in Yucatan, and lived in Boston from 1962 to 1964. Has published more than 30 books mostly about the Mayan history, literature and mythology. Has written narratives, chronicles, newspaper reports and literary essays. He also has translated several historical and literary works from English to Spanish. Obtained the *Premio Estatal de Literatura Antonio Meriz Bolio* (Literature State Award) in 1992 and the *Medalla* Yucatan in 2011.

The stories herein are by writers who -- far removed from the countries of their birth- share their views on many aspects of this culture; learning a new language and finding joy in the simpler life. This is their Yucatan-from their hearts!

Reg Deneau ~ Author of *Trust the Winds-Poems of a Spiritual Journey*

It is delightful to read in a light, easy and well-edited manner the adventures and vicissitudes of these writers, my good friends, who have kindly chosen the state of Yucatan in Mexico as their new home. A book containing a variety of laughs, of awkward or difficult situations, which made me enjoy and made me see my own surroundings, so natural to me, from a very different and agreeable viewpoint. Thank you, friends, for sharing your experience with the world. This is a book that I am sure will be of public interest. Congratulations.
Maricarmen Perez ~ Appointed International Ambassador of Yucatecan Music. Musician, singer and traditional and folklore music investigator. Cultural coordinator at the Secretariat of Culture and Arts in Yucatan.

Uniquely Yucatan is a colorful literary patchwork quilt of ex-pat life in the Yucatan. And, like a patchwork quilt made from cloth remnants, a close look at the pieces gives insight into the lives of the makers. In this case it is immediately obvious that the writers do not live in the bubble of gated communities or within the comfort zone of largely English speaking communities. Here you will encounter a collection of real (and some not so real–but illustrative) tales which range from Maya mysticism to the nitty gritty potholes of life, customs and language while living in Mexico. I have to confess – some were so funny I still have tears of laughter in my eyes as I type this. If you are north-of-the border and are contemplating a richer and more interesting life south of it – or, for that matter, even if you aren't – I would highly recommend *Uniquely Yucatan*. It will enrich your life.
Robert E. Jack ~ Author of *Sailing with Rhyme and Reason* and former resident of the Yucatan Peninsula, Mexico.

Uniquely Yucatan

**STORIES AND POEMS
MOSTLY TRUE,
SPICED WITH
ARTISTIC LICENSE**

THE MERIDA
WRITERS' GROUP

Uniquely Yucatan:
Stories and poems mostly true, spiced with artistic license

Copyright © 2015 by each member of Merida Writers' Group.
All rights reserved.

ISBN 13: 978-1519232960
ISBN 10: 151-9232969

Cover Photography: © Cherie Pittillo
Cover Design: Jeanine Henning
Editors: Gwen Lane, Maryetta Ackenbom
Interior Layout: Maureen Cutajar

Dedicated to the storyteller in every soul.

May our written words inspire and warm hearts through all the days of life.

Acknowledgements

We would like to thank the Secretariat of Culture and Arts for the State of Yucatan and the board and staff at the Merida English Library for their continued support and encouragement.

Our appreciation to Ignacio Duran Encalada of *Mosaicas La Peninsular* for sharing his knowledge of the colorful pasta tiles and a uniquely Yucatan treasure with us.

Hugs to all the unique people and situations that inspire us.

Contents

Introduction	1
Gwen Lane	
Uniquely Yucatan	3
Gwen Lane	
What's in a Name?	11
Cherie Pittillo	
Yucatan Triptych	15
Maryetta Ackenbom	
Flamingo Revenge	21
Lorraine Baillie Bowie	
Speaking Spanish While Gringo	27
Theresa Diaz Gray	
Sallie's Gift	31
Lorna Gail Dallin	
La Peregrina	37
Maryetta Ackenbom	

To Xocen [show – ken]	39
Lorna Gail Dallin	
He Lives With Me	47
Theresa Diaz Gray	
What I Meant to Say	49
Lorraine Baillie Bowie	
A Sustainable Tradition	55
Cherie Pittillo	
Yucatan Sol	67
Gwen Lane	
The Burning Season	69
Maryetta Ackenbom	
Creature of Shadow and Sun: Snowy Egret	75
Cherie Pittillo	
Artist's Palette	77
Cherie Pittillo	
The Queen of Mexico	79
Lorna Gail Dallin	
The Cross in the Tree	87
Maryetta Ackenbom	
A Very Mérida Christmas	91
Theresa Diaz Gray	
My Line Full of Memories	99
Cherie Pittillo	
Time Divine or Define Time	103
Gwen Lane	

A Woman of a Certain Age	109
Lorraine Baillie Bowie	
Blanche and the Big Cry	111
Lorna Gail Dallin	
Wren Ovation	117
Cherie Pittillo	
On the Beach	119
Maryetta Ackenbom	
The Encounter	125
Gwen Lane	
Roswell to Merida	127
Lorraine Baillie Bowie	
How Not to Social Network	139
Cherie Pittillo	
Frances and the False Friends	141
Theresa Diaz Gray	
Things that Make Me Smile in Merida	151
Cherie Pittillo	
Crickets and Cheese Please	153
Gwen Lane	
Saltator with a Side of Greens	159
Cherie Pittillo	
The Ruins	163
Maryetta Ackenbom	
Runaway Bride	171
Cherie Pittillo	

Yucatan Yogis	175
Gwen Lane	
War Hero or "Rat with Wings"?	181
Cherie Pittillo	
Gringo Conspiracy	185
Lorraine Baillie Bowie	
Broken Rainbow	193
Cherie Pittillo	
Chainsaws and Homeless	195
Cherie Pittillo	
Owlet	199
Maryetta Ackenbom	
Scrambled Breakfast	203
Gwen Lane	
An Embarrassing Moment...	209
Lorna Gail Dallin	
The Neophyte Birdwatcher	213
Maryetta Ackenbom	
A Cat Burglar from the Get Go? No, a Gecko!	217
Cherie Pittillo	
The Wandering Iguanas	219
Gwen Lane	
State of Yucaland	225
Gwen Lane	

GWEN LANE

Introduction

The essence of a writer is woven within the written words and together they form a tapestry of tales and fabrics of fiction that touch souls.

In this book we have uncovered more secrets and unique treasures of Yucatan to tickle your heart and touch your funny bones.

You will meet a multi-generational Yucatan family that protects and preserves an old growth forest and sacred land that supports and sustains them.

Discover the unique gift from Yucatan to the world.

Laugh along with us as we share our blunders and missteps in coping with a new language and different customs.

We tell of our personal and sometimes up close animal experiences with the unique and diverse wildlife that traverses our Yucatan.

And you will find enough Maya mysticism to make you stop and wonder at the meaning of it all.

We featured handcrafted Yucatan embroidery on the cover of our first book, *Our Yucatan*. For **Uniquely Yucatan**, we chose the handmade colorful pasta floor tiles.

In some ways our lives are like the handmade tiles and hand embroidery clothing, uniquely individual and yet similar. Together stitch by stitch or tile by tile a design of our life is woven into the fabric of our spirit. The chips and scars are witness to the wear life has put upon us, the cost of experience and our ability to still shine uniquely.

An occasional face lift of deep cleaning and polishing gives the tiles and ourselves strength and radiance to endure the weight of the load placed upon us.

We hope you find our stories and writings a face lifting experience, that brightens your way, helps you to shine, and touches your soul.

The Merida Writers' Group
Maryetta, Rainie, Lorna Gail, Cherie, Theresa, Gwen

GWEN LANE

Uniquely Yucatan

Secrets. I wanted to hear secrets when Maryetta and I sat down to interview the owner of Mosaicos La Peninsular, Ignacio Duran Encalada. (He doesn't mind if you call him "Nacho".) His smooth tanned skin and agile physique suggest a man years younger than one thinking about retirement. I asked him to tell us something most people don't know about the uniquely Yucatan pasta tiles.

"Oh," he smiled wide with a wink in his voice, "the tiles have many secrets. If I told you, they wouldn't be secrets. But, I can tell you that each and every tile is handmade. We use the highest quality craftsmanship, molds and materials. Our tiles contain an essence of the artist within them."

A flow of energy between the materials and the crafter enhances its allure and gives it an intriguing and unique character.

The beauty, essence and bright colors lured Nacho in 1989 to purchase a plant that had stopped making tiles, as had many companies in the area at that time. This factory had been making twelve by twelve inch tiles with less color and designs and easier to fabricate than the tiles made there now.

Nacho gave us a little history of this Merida business on Calle 62. "This shop got started back in 1970, and I got here nineteen years later, in November 1989. The name of the business has remained the same through the years, Mosaicos La Peninsular."

Nacho bought the business on a downswing in popularity of the pasta tiles. Ceramic, marble, granite, and porcelains had entered the flooring market.

He and his family have worked hard and struggled to build a quality business and survived hard times. The 1995 economic downturn and Hurricane Isadora, in 2002, he remembered as particularly bad times.

His positive outlook and feeling of connection with life show how he survived, "Times of crisis can be times of opportunity and I feel fortunate. Shortly after I bought the business, the baby boomers from the north found their way to the Yucatan."

Their enchantment with the pasta tiles helped his business to grow. Good English skills learned while he attended school for a year in New Buffalo, Michigan, when he was seventeen, gave him the advantage in helping English speakers.

Nacho was born in Merida, Yucatan, and has spent most of his life here. He started his career as a mechanical engineer for a large company in Mexico City but he "always wanted something to call my own".

I asked what attracted him to the business. With warmth in his face that complemented his salt and pepper hair and comfortable easy manner, he replied, "Pasta tiles are beautiful, full of bright colors. Something the makers of other tiles have not been able to duplicate. The market here is turning back to a preference for the pasta tiles. We are making the tiles the exact same way they were made one hundred and fifty years ago or more. It's a handcraft."

He continued sharing the process, "the only difference now is the pressing of the tiles. Today we use hydraulic pressure, thanks to electricity. But in the old days they had no electricity, no compressors. They had to press the tiles by mechanical weight, with a big lever or big screw. Using hydraulic pressure has helped to make better tiles because they are more even and pressed tighter." He stressed that this is the only thing that has changed through the years.

For many years the pasta tiles were called hydraulic tiles. Ah ha, a secret, I knew I could get one. But, maybe not, because Nacho says, "In Spain they still refer to them as hydraulic tiles and when I bought the business you could still read on the façade, *Mosaicos Hidraulicos*," (Hydraulic Tiles).

He explained his business ideals that have helped him succeed. "We put our heart and soul in this job. I come here very early in the morning. I open, and I see all the workers come in and make sure things get started and done properly and everything is right. If there is a problem, we can solve it at the moment. We take much care of the quality of the tiles. We check every tile before it leaves our shop. If there is a major error, we pull it aside."

Nacho says minor imperfections are acceptable and give the tiles character, and add personality to a home or building. I like his ease with the world. "The perfect is the enemy of the good. We cannot always expect perfection in our lives but we should always expect the good of life."

Maryetta asked Nacho how the Talavera tiles differ from the pasta tiles.

"The Talavera tiles are painted on the top of the tile and baked. Pasta tiles have no heat, no smoke, they are a green product. The pasta is part of the tile and the paint colors are part of the tile."

Nacho, in his relaxed approach continued with more things that set his pasta tiles apart from the rest. "Another interesting and finely detailed handcraft is making the molds."

Nacho buys and cuts the sheets of copper and gives them along with a design on paper to a local artist who makes the molds. A simple mold could cost about 2500 pesos, plus tax. Anyone could have an artisan make a unique mold design.

"Most of the tiles are replications of the old, old designs. We have recovered them from old houses." He has a wall in his showroom of 35 different tile designs they want to restore. "Every different design takes a different mold and it is very time consuming and costly. Iron tile was what was brought over on the ships from Spain. We are making an imitation of that tile."

Nacho continued to taunt me with the secrets. "Of course, there are many secrets about making the tiles. Sometimes people come here to see how the tiles are done and they think it is easy. The people we have make it look easy, but it is not. Making the tiles isn't something you learn at University. It is a handcraft and does have many secrets.

"I learned a lot of my secrets from one of the previous owners who had many years of experience and he agreed to stay a month after I bought the business and train me. I was fortunate that many of the experienced employees wanted to stay and I continued learning from them."

His most memorable job would have to be the *xocbichuy* carpet, (unique embroidery cross stitch design made with pasta tiles) at the Maya museum. Xocbichuy in the Mayan language means cross stitch as it is used in the handmade Yucatecan dresses. He feels it is one of their best works. For a long time he could not figure out how to make the unique clothing carpet design. He spent many restless nights and lay awake thinking how to do it right.

"Not easy because unlike the other tiles, each one of these tiles is different. This tile has to be made upside down, we have to make it backwards and when people gave me the plan, I had to make one drawing for every different tile. I had to use a mirror to see to make the pattern upside down. I got a piece of paper and put the color by hand, different color in every different square. It was very difficult to do.

"Today we can make it much easier with the computers. But at the time I made this carpet I didn't use the computer. So, I had to rack my mind, figuring out how to do it, for many long hours."

Maryetta asked if there was much demand for the xocbichuy Maya carpets.

"It's funny, but this kind of tile doesn't appeal much too North Americans and Europeans. My son says, half joking and half-truth, that they see it as a simple pixel. They are so technologically advanced that maybe they look at this as a pixel picture. That might be one reason you don't like it very much but people in the Yucatan, they do like it very much.

"It is expensive because every tile is different from the others; it takes long hours to make them. But this is a gift from the Yucatan to the world."

He has investigated different tile sites in countries all over the world—Vietnam, Spain, Morocco, Cuba and others. There are factories still making the pasta tiles but he hasn't seen any of them making this xocbichuy kind of carpet work.

"This is Uniquely Yucatan." His overall visage radiates his pride of accomplishment and with eyes filled with an inner glow he proclaims," We have enriched a little bit the pasta tile designs with this kind of work of the xocbichuy Maya carpets."

The Maya carpet work of Nacho and his dedicated team can be seen at the *Gran Museo del Mundo Maya*, The Peregrina Hotel on

Calle 51 between 58 y 56, Hotel Itza on 59 close to the Congress Building, and some haciendas.

Business is good right now and they have taken orders from all over Mexico. They have sent tiles to Los Cabos on the Pacific Coast, and shipped orders to Belize and Panama.

Nacho says, "We have too much work right now. I am fortunate because we just bought a factory four miles from here from a North American who thought making these tiles was easy. They had many technical problems because, like I told you, the tiles have many secrets. Right now we are redoing and reorganizing the factory, cleaning and making things right so we can have good quality."

He plans on eventually spending less time at the business and his two sons are interested in carrying on this traditional tile work.

As we finished the interview I heard music behind the closed doors of the factory on the other side of the showroom. I asked if we might look inside for a moment. Maryetta paid close attention to the tile making process while I spoke with Nacho about his happy crew.

Many times when I have visited Mosaicos La Peninsular, I heard laughter and music coming from the shop. On my last visit Hungarian dance music filled my ears complete with shouting, foot stomping and tool banging at the appropriate times. I wanted to throw up my arms and glide across the floor and stacks of tiles. I could sense the energy and vibration within. He smiled wide and gave an easy nod. "Happy employees do better work." I had to agree.

Maryetta shares her impressions of watching a tile being made:

I don't plan to reveal any of Nacho's secrets—I don't know any. This is what I observed:

For each tile, the base of the copper form is divided into sections, each section meant to hold a paste with the color assigned to that section. The worker squeezes the colored paste into each division as you would icing on a cake. After each division is filled with the appropriate colored paste, a powder is sprinkled like flour over the whole, until all the colors are completely covered, and then handfuls of the same powder fill the form to a certain level. On top of this, a different powder is spread until it reaches the top of the form. It's evened off, and the entire form is placed in the hydraulic press. A couple of minutes later, the form is removed, and the completed tile is taken from the form, the bottom becoming the top. It's dusted off and inspected, and exhibited to the breathless observer.

∞

Have you ever seen something so attractive, so stunning, you don't dare touch it? Let alone step all over it with shoe grime and dirt. And yet that is what these magnificent pieces of art are for. Perhaps as we step across these floors some of the love and essence of the crafter fills us with energy, hope and creativity. Perhaps we leave some essence of ourselves on the tiles we transverse.

Take time in your life for your heart, light and energy to blend and something unique will be created.

CHERIE PITTILLO

What's in a Name?

When my husband and I moved to Merida, Yucatan, Mexico, we knew some of the benefits and disadvantages of living in a country different from the United States of America. One of the disadvantages was not speaking the Spanish language of our new country. However, one benefit we learned about quickly was our local *tienda,* the tiny 7-11- like convenience store. Located in Santiago, this store on the corner of Calle 70 and 51 had the long name of *La Preferida, tienda de abarrotes (*the preferred store of groceries).

Equipped with my pesos in cash and *cambio* (change), I went to buy cleaning supplies. Since I had enrolled in a Spanish class soon after our arrival, I tried out my new expressions. The proprietor spoke English and said he could help me with Spanish. I asked his name and heard him say, "Gustavo."

His mom assisted him in the tienda unless the heat bothered her. Then she relaxed in a hammock behind the cashier counter.

I've been amazed at that little store and what I found in it. Two inch cellophane sacks held peppercorns or cinnamon. I could buy one aspirin or one egg. This, like most tiendas, will sell single items. When you need something, the tienda clerk will do anything possible to help you. Light bulbs, toothbrushes, cough drops, and unfamiliar names initially greeted me. *Zote, Totopos, Axion.* Now I know those names and their uses whether I use those brands or not.

How interesting to me that I learned those names and then got a shock at MY tienda.

I received a phone call in English from Gustavo. Sure I had my cell phone minutes recharged there. And he's a nice guy, but why would he telephone me for the first time in five years unless something was wrong?

"Hola, is this Cherie?"

"Yes, it is."

"When will you be in Celestun?"

"May I ask who's calling?"

"Gustavo."

"Would you repeat that please?"

"Yes, my name is Gustavo."

"Gustavo?"

"Yes, Gustavo."

"Is everything okay? Why are you calling me from Celestun?"

"Because you rented a room here. You come *en la tarde* (in the afternoon). Yes?"

I thought," Okay, I understand now; the clerk's name at the hotel was Gustavo."

"Si, si. Yes, today at 3 pm," I replied.

"*Gracias! Hasta luego.*"

"Gracias, Gustavo. Hasta luego."

WHAT'S IN A NAME?

After my overnight birding trip to Celestun, I returned to my favorite tienda and told Gustavo that I thought he called me. I repeated the phone conversation. He looked down as he said, "My name is not Gustavo."

I said, "Yes it is."

He said, "No, it isn't."

I said "Yes, it is."

He shook his head no.

I replied again, "Yes it is. E*s broma.* (it's a joke)."

"No, my name is not Gustavo."

Dumbfounded, I asked, "What IS your name?"

He said, "Gonzalo."

"Gonzalo?"

"Yes, Gonzalo. My name is Gonzalo."

Then I asked, "Why did you let me and my husband call you 'Gustavo' for five years?"

"I didn't want to upset you."

That conversation is a great example of the people of Yucatan. How they value tranquility and peace. How they don't want to confront, even when it comes to a name.

What I didn't misunderstand is that every few months for five years I thanked Gonzalo for the community service he has provided to so many people. Almost every time I went into the tienda, locals were in the store. He and his mother open from 7:30 AM, close from 2-5 PM and reopen from 5-7 PM, every day except holidays, five and a half days a week. They hardly ever took a vacation.

For several years I had called him Gustavo, and I apologized. Then when I learned his name, I'd call him Gustavo-Gonzalo.

And now I say, "Gonzalo, my friend, my amigo".

[13]

MARYETTA ACKENBOM

Yucatan Triptych

I. Heat

Hot. Sweat poured over me so fast that I had to shower and change my blouse at least three times a day. Antiperspirant was useless. And it was only April!

I didn't remember it being that hot a few years ago. Age takes its toll. The thermometer read over 90 degrees Fahrenheit.

I brought it on myself, of course, by retiring to a semitropical climate. But I had no regrets.

When I was fifteen years old, I experienced pain, real pain, traipsing through a snowy countryside with friends in eastern Kansas. I decided right then that if I had a choice, I'd never live in a cold climate again.

In college a few years later, I was snowbound in a bus in Nebraska with the rest of the college choir. We all trudged through the painful icy stuff for half-a-mile to a nearby house to save ourselves from freezing until the bus got dug out. My resolve to move south was fortified.

My sister recently sent me a gorgeous photograph of an azalea bush in front of her house in Denver, in full bloom and covered with snow. She called the picture "Easter in Colorado." I just shivered.

When I passed the U.S. Foreign Service examination, in my long-ago youth, I filled out an assignment preference list. Some of my colleagues advised me to fill out the places I did not want to go, and then I'd surely not be sent there. I'd always been a little contrary. I wrote "Tropical Africa" in the space provided.

When I stepped off the plane in Abidjan, Ivory Coast, a few months later, a unique odor came to my nostrils. Others later identified it for me—a combination of damp heat, dust rising from the pavement, rotting vegetation, and unwashed bodies. For some reason, I didn't find it unpleasant. I was comfortable in the tropics.

After two blessed years, I was assigned back to Washington, D.C., where I suffered through one of the coldest winters ever known there. I volunteered for assignment to the Embassy in Saigon, knowing that with the war on there, few others would be on the volunteer list. Sure enough, it gave me another year and a half of pleasant warmth. I dodged a few bullets, took a few risky plane and helicopter rides, but I was content.

As a reward, my leaders sent me to Paris. Cold, rainy, miserable Paris. Forget April in Paris. Only August is tolerable, when all the Parisians leave town for the beaches in the south. I walked all over the city—the only way I could keep warm!

After another eternity in Washington, D.C., studying Spanish, I went off to Mexico City. I was happy at first, until the first winter in the high plateau hit me and I coughed all the way to the Embassy building three blocks away from my apartment. I took my first opportunity and ran with it—a temporary duty assignment in Merida, Yucatan. Merida is approximately on the same latitude as Mexico City, but it's at sea level and gets cold—actually, cool—only about two weeks of the year. I could live with that. I parlayed the two months temporary duty into a regular assignment.

Two years there, a stint in Washington and in Miami, then retirement and back to Merida. It was hot. But I was happy.

II. Locusts

Whispering, "ticka-ticka-ticka."

I looked up, and then quickly stepped away from the tree. Hordes, swarms, gazillions of the varmints were up in my lime tree yesterday, chomping away, letting fall little bits of green and little bits of excrement. The raspy whispers came from jaws, working away to destroy my wonderful tree.

The locusts began to arrive last week. Only a few at first, maybe a dozen. My terriers chased them down. The insects seemed to be blind, running into walls and doors, falling to the ground and immediately taking off again, sometimes butting their heads against the same wall time and again, giving the dogs a great chance to catch them. The bugs were about two inches long, some longer; a great opportunity for the dogs to hone their hunting instincts.

The next day a few more appeared. Maybe fifty.

Then, after that day, I realized I was in trouble. Multiplied trouble.

In this hot, dry season I have to leave doors open, and the dogs run in and out of the house, into the walled yard, as they please. Soon they began bringing in their catches and massacring them on my floor. The house became a locust mortuary. Many, not quite dead, hopped lamely around the floor until the dogs caught up with them again.

In the evening the beasts came in by themselves, swarming around any light I had on. By that time I had given up. Useless to sweep and clean; in an hour or two there would again be hordes on the floor.

The local newspaper had warned of the approaching locust swarms a couple of months ago. Then, about three or four weeks ago, I witnessed two incredibly dense throngs passing over the city. They covered the sun like a cloud, shading the streets below. What is bigger than a gazillion? There must be a word. In their convent yard nearby a group of nuns started pounding kettles and pans, making a tremendous racket. They explained that the plague would not land if they made enough noise until the entire horde had passed.

Last night I asked my neighbor, "What can we do?"

He only said, "Wait."

So I am waiting, cringing in my house, and looking sadly at the bare branches of my trees and plants. It's too late to pound on kettles and pans. My littlest dog is sitting by my side, exhausted from the hunt, just watching the huge hoppers bounding around her.

III. Rain

In Yucatan, there is a rainy season and a dry season. The rains usually don't amount to a monsoon, but they are plentiful, and typically last about an hour or two a day, for three months. The dry season is not as dry as a desert, but temperatures are quite high and the gardens shrivel.

YUCATAN TRIPTYCH

The mildest season of the year is from about October, when the rains are definitely ending, to the end of March. Then the lack of rain begins to be felt, with spring and summer rapidly approaching. By the middle of May, we are all suffering.

Then in June, more or less, the blessed rains begin. They are blessed for a week or two, and then cursed for the incursions they make on private plans.

Today is May 19. We have suffered an extremely hot dry spell for more than three weeks. But now it is raining!

I had just told my panting dogs, "Wouldn't it be wonderful if it rained?" I must have heard the first pit-pat of the drops on the big philodendron leaves outside my window. When I identified the sound, I ran out the door, the dogs bounding after me. We all got thoroughly drenched.

I lifted my mouth to the heavens and spread my arms wide to welcome the pure rainwater. Somewhat pure—farmers have been burning wasteland for crops, and the air was full of ash, which made the heat more unbearable and made the rain run ashily into the gutter. But it felt grand!

LORRAINE BAILLIE BOWIE

Flamingo Revenge

Roger and I charged into Yucatan in our white Blazer, overstuffed with remnants of our previous life. I left much behind in Texas, but I, unfortunately, held onto a personality trait I spent a lifetime trying to conquer. Little Miss Know-it-all appeared in childhood and, though she served me well in some aspects of my life, she has played havoc during times of stress. I try to suppress this bossy attitude, but when I am tense or worried; she jumps to the surface and takes over my mind and body.

In Progreso for only one week and sporting zero language skills, I was, of course, tense and worried, a cue for Miss Know-it-all to emerge. I dragged a reluctant Roger to Spanish class where we met first- time Yucatan visitors, Canadians Peggy and Richard, our very first English speaking friends. Miss Know-it-all studied with frenzy in an attempt to conquer her fears of adjusting to a culture as new as the first day of Kindergarten, but without the benefit of a shared language.

The four of us newbies became fast friends and set out to explore the countryside. Finding flamingos was our first obsession. My homeland experience with flamingos was limited to the garden variety cheap plastic rendition of this elegant bird. I confess that I demeaned and disenfranchised this famous fowl by buying an entire flock at Wal-Mart garden center. That night, crouching in the glow of landscape lighting and with crickets chirping encouragement, I assisted my husband to relocate the flock of phonies to a neighbor's front yard. For months, our upscale neighborhood, with its rigid rules against yard art, was held hostage by its homeowners moving the flock from house to house. Any Miss or Mr. Know-it-all will identify with my mixed feelings about my participation in the flamingo caper. Although thrilled to collaborate in the conspiracy, my hands trembled under the weight of a growing guilt over using one of God's glorious creatures to perpetuate an illegal neighborhood escapade. I had a feeling my short life of perpetrating criminal flamingo yard art would come back to bite me and, years later in the Yucatan, it did.

With the men in the front seat to ward off danger and women in the back to direct the men, we set off on our self-proclaimed flamingo safari. With our snow white hair, winter-white North American complexion, and white Blazer we looked like four Q-tips stuck in a marshmallow.

Our Spanish teacher, Raphael, assured us we would find flamingos if we followed the road going east. "If you drive along the Gulf, you will find a viewing tower with binoculars for rent." Now, finally, I could erase the shame of my former flamingo abuse by viewing, honoring and admiring this majestic bird in its natural habitat.

Having traveled much further than Rafael indicated and finding no flamingos, we, in the back seat, considered the possibility that we may be lost. The men in the front ignored our pleas to stop for directions.

Peggy leaned toward my left ear and, covering her mouth with her hand, mumbled, "I don't care what country a man is from, they will never ask for directions and will never admit to being lost."

"Peggy," I responded in a voice for all to hear, "men are never lost; they may be, at times, temporarily misdirected, but never confused or bewildered about their location."

Passing through pueblo after pueblo, the men further strengthened their masculine identity by refusing to ask for directions. An hour and a half later, signs we couldn't read grew further apart; the road dwindled to one lane, overhung with the jungle attempting to take back its land. A lush smell of moss replaced the tangy smell of the Gulf. Seductive sounds drew us deeper into the bush and further away from our reality and comfort zone. I watched streams of brilliant blue fighting for passage through the dense canopy of trees.

Breaking himself out of his tropical daze, commonly referred to as tranquility, Roger glanced back in my direction and said, "I give up. Miss Know-it-all, if you know the Spanish name for flamingos, I'll ask for directions."

⁂

After making a snarky remark that we had gone so deep into the jungle that only an expert in the Mayan language could help us, I agreed to supply the phrase in Spanish. In class, we practiced saying, "I want..." and " Where is...?" How hard could this be? If only I could remember the Spanish name for flamingos.

"I have it," I said, "It's flamboyanes—I'm sure of it." If I had taken a moment to look up flamboyanes, I would have found a magnificent tree with fiery red blossoms, not a flamingo. Due to my insistence and the lack of other options, the three deferred to my feigned expertise. We agreed that we would ask the very next person we saw. When Roger rolled down the window to make ready for his Spanish language debut, a swarm of buzzing and energetic mosquitoes filled the car.

After several unproductive language exchanges, that resulted in us becoming even more lost, covered with mosquito bites, and leaving local residents wide-eyed in our wake, we came upon a man standing at a crossroads. I thought he must be waiting for a bicycle taxi as the road was not large enough for a bus. The Blazer still suffers from unhealed jungle scratches. Roger rolled down his window and again asked, "Donde esta flamboyanes?"

A familiar puzzled expression crossed the man's face. Roger ruffled my feathers when he again glanced in my direction as if to ask if I was sure about the translation. Irritated at the implied question, I said, "Roger, flamboyanes is correct. No doubt your pronunciation is at fault."

This time Roger refused to give up. He repeated the word over and over as if repetition would help his pronunciation. Determined to be understood, Roger leaned out of the passenger window. The man moved closer but appeared ready to run if we should exit the vehicle. Roger leaned further out the window and flailed his arms like an enormous white bird in distress. "Flamboyanes, flamboyanes" he called out while flapping his arms even faster. His face turned pink, causing me to worry about his blood pressure.

After hesitating a moment, the puzzled expression on the man's face gave way to a look of recognition. He took another step forward and readied himself to speak. I knew how difficult it must be to have to communicate with us, so I too leaned out of my window in case my assistance may be needed.

I was willing to do whatever I could to make up for disenfranchising those plastic flamingos.

He moved forward to within six inches of Roger's pink perspiring face and, in perfect English, said, "Would you perhaps mean flamingos?"

THERESA DIAZ GRAY

Speaking Spanish While Gringo

Our physical appearances subtly affect many interactions in ways that we don't think about when we live NOB (north of the border). Then we move here and it hits us between the eyes. Taxis will pass Yucatecans to pick up my husband, especially in Cancun. The same taxi drivers will give me a better fare than him if there is no meter.

My husband is over six feet tall, fair-skinned, and blue-eyed. Even though most of his hair is brown, the portion that shows in front is white as is his neatly trimmed beard. When he was heavier, little kids in the park often would call out, "Santa Claus," when they saw him. Now that he is slim again, the comparisons to Saint Nick have stopped, but strangers still don't expect him to speak any Spanish. Speaking Spanish while gringo is a phenomenon that leads to more frustration for my husband than almost anything else that happens to him here. His Spanish vocabulary is limited, but his accent and sentence construction are excellent. He is very easy to understand when he speaks Spanish.

Regardless of his language abilities, an interesting scene is played out whenever we eat at a new restaurant. The waiter inquires what we'd like to drink. My husband answers, "*Quisiera tomar una limonada por favor,*" asking for a lemonade.

The waiter does his best deer in the headlights impression and blurts out, "*¿Una cerveza?*"

Years ago, I would immediately jump in to help, explaining, "*Mi esposo pidió una limonada,*" my husband asked for a lemonade. Now, I wait until it sinks in that my husband is speaking Spanish or let him handle it himself.

After being here for many years, I have finally figured out what is going on. As the server approaches our table he spots my husband, immediately identifies him as a foreigner. I can hear his internal dialog now. "*Oh, no, that man doesn't speak Spanish, what will I do? I won't understand him. What do foreigners drink? Oh, yes, a beer, foreigners drink beer.*" The waiter is so busy worrying about what might happen that he doesn't hear what beverage my husband actually requests.

I have the opposite problem; everyone assumes that I am Mexican until I open my mouth. I am tall for a Yucatecan, but I am short for an American. Furthermore, I have what I call standard Mediterranean looks, even with my silver hair. When I speak, they don't know what to think. One of my cousins once told me that I have the most mixed up accent she ever heard.

"Sometimes you sound Cuban, sometimes Spanish, and other times pure American. Why is that?" she asked me.

My answer is that it depends upon where I learned the word in question. Now, I am sure that I also have added some Yucatecan and Mexican flavor to my accent. The words with which I have the most problems are those that are spelled the same in both languages or have been co-opted by English. Even though my parents are Cuban immigrants, we mostly spoke English at home. In California, where I grew up, Spanish was mandatory in the 6th, 7th and 8th grades. In high school it was optional so while I did take it my freshman year, I opted for Latin my sophomore year. In college, I made it through Intermediate Spanish. I felt prepared for living in Mexico.

Sometimes when I am out and about, I either forget the Spanish word for something, or use a different word than they use here. For example, I needed a zipper. The word I grew up using for zipper is zipper said with a Spanish accent. Convinced that wouldn't be correct, I looked it up. The term used in Spain is *cremallera*. When I asked the salesgirl for one, she looked very blankly at me. I tried, *zee-per*, no luck. Finally, I pantomimed opening and closing a pants zipper. She brightened up and said, "*Un cierre*," cierre literally means closure. Then she peered at me quizzically and asked, "You aren't from here are you?" She obviously was wondering if I was from some remote *pueblito* where they don't have zippers or if perhaps I suffered from Alzheimer's syndrome.

The politest way that I have ever been asked about my accent is, "What part of Mexico are you from?" I was flattered but answered, "Hearing me speak Spanish, do you really think I am Mexican?"

One day, I answered the door wearing what I call my *abuelita* (grandma) uniform, an embroidered housecoat and flip flops. A group of Jehovah's Witnesses congregated on my doorstep. They spoke to me in Spanish so I answered them in Spanish.

"Good afternoon, we understand that the people who live here speak English."

I simply replied, "Yes," while wondering at their novel approach.

"We would like to speak English with the owners of the house," the speaker for the group announced while looking at me expectantly.

Speechless, I processed this odd statement and waited for the conversation to continue in English. We looked at each other in silence until it dawned upon me that they thought that I was the maid, and were waiting for me to fetch the foreigners. Finally, in slow and careful English I answered them, "Everyone in this household speaks English including the dog. Did you want to talk to him?" as I closed the door on their astonished faces. We weren't bothered with any more Jehovah's Witnesses for about a month after that.

When *Mijo* (an affectionate contraction of *mi hijo*, my son) lived here, the fastest way home from his bus stop lead through the main square. Like my husband, he is tall but has my Latin looks. Mexicans think he looks either Cuban or Argentine, most tourists assume he is Mexican. He smiles easily and dressed in his school uniform of gray slacks and white guayabera gives off an air of middle class respectability. Often sightseers would approach him asking if he spoke English. Hearing his California accent, many of them would then want to know, "Where did you learn English?" He quickly found that informing them, "I am an American," lead to more personal questions than he was comfortable with. Eventually he changed his answer to, "I studied in the States when I was younger," which allowed him to continue home to his after school snack in a timelier manner. Now that he is back in California, Spanish speakers he encounters often ask him if he is from Michoacán.

Sometimes, when my husband and I are out and about, we spot people who look like they might be native English speakers but we know that they probably aren't. What you see is not always what you get here.

LORNA GAIL DALLIN

Sallie's Gift

My friend Sallie feels the hounds of mortality nipping at her heels. She instructs me; "Come to my house – I need you to help me do something ... NOW!" She calls me to her house in Chuburna, a northern suburb of Merida, to put names of family members on the backs of her wonderfully eclectic collection of framed "things" ... art and artefact, wall hangings. Sallie is in her 80's so her collection is beautifully aged.

I write down a name on a small sticky label which she produces from her stationery supply drawer, procured especially for this task no doubt, and at first the procedure is rather perfunctory ... a name and a point with her cane to the piece to which she wants the sticky attached. Nothing is said about why she chooses as she does but she is quick about it. She has thought through this distribution and knows what she wants. Well, that pretty much describes Sallie herself.

Soon, there are only two pieces not yet designated. From her wheelchair and with her cane, Sallie points to one piece. It is a smallish, black framed pen and ink drawing of several Maya glyphs. At least knowing Sallie, I assume them to be Maya.

"I want you to have this one," she says "I know you are interested in the Maya days and if I remember correctly, those are all day glyphs. I got that on a trip to Chiapas." She moves on to the next piece, a delicate watercolour rendering of a small bird on a flower stem and says, "That one is for my son-in-law, Bruce."

―・―

One summer, several years ago, I partook of a session of teachings on the Maya Calendar days, looking at the Tzolkin calendar. A charismatic instructor and leading authority on Chichen Itza and the pyramid of K'u-Kuul-Kaan was our guide. The teachings that the Tzolkin calendar might provide intrigued me. It is a ritual calendar of 13 "months", each month is 20 days. The span of one round or "year" is then, 260 days. Each month consists of the same 20 days. I also began to notice that as I visited each of the 20 days, I was becoming more and more familiar with the distinct glyph for each day. I found myself looking for them on visits to Maya sites and often recognized some of the glyphs when used in decorative art pieces. I came to learn that the Maya put some store by the day on which a person is born. Each of the twenty days has practical aspects and wisdom attached to it and that informs the character of a person born on that day.

I put the 20 glyphs together with my class notes recalling what was addressed on each day including which cardinal direction was assigned to each Maya day, giving each day a distinct venue. This fit wonderfully with my own circle meditations which I enjoy each morning in my garden. In the months following this come together of information on the calendar, I set out to follow a Tzolkin ritual "year", reading each day the wisdom and instruction accorded it.

I make no claims about my interpretations of this material and what the Maya might call the real thing. My reflections came from a heart-based teacher, through the sensibilities of a seeker who used the thoughts of each Maya day to craft a body of ideas, reflections and insight that created a focus for the day. It is wonderfully helpful to have something to contemplate each day; and to have the opportunity to revisit the thoughts of a day to see what they have to offer each time you encounter them. My motto through these daily reflections has been: "I do not seek to unlock the secrets of the Maya, rather, to unlock the secrets of myself." Such has been the case. I have had numerous rich insights into myself, my community, and the binary mind through my contemplations of this ritual calendar. Often a phrase from these reflections will drop into my consciousness at some point in a day. These come at appropriate moments and are generally clear to me. Sometimes I have to search for some relevance or application and the results can either give me an Aha! ... or, a ha ha ha.

∞

I thank Sallie for her thoughtful gesture, her gift, and we move on from the hanging things which are now all designated, to the book shelves. On her very first trip to the Yucatan, while she and husband Doug were still living in Chicago, Sallie fell under the sway of the Maya and their ancient world. She developed into a true "maya-ist", visiting all the "known" sites, large, small, no matter how difficult to access. After they moved to Merida, Sallie visited them all with her trusty companion Douglas, who liked to talk with the gatekeepers and visitors while Sallie walked and climbed the sites. She had over the years collected an impressive array of scholarly books written about the Maya. Sallie wanted these books to go to her alma mater and that had been arranged. She pointed all this out to me as we surveyed her material world. When she tired, I was given a glimpse into the closet where all the important papers were stored, and then was instructed to go home.

When Sallie dies a week later, we clean out her home of all her material reminders and disburse them according to her directions. I bring the small black framed glyphs drawing home with me along with two urns containing the ashes of Sallie and of Douglas, who died almost exactly one year previously. A promise has been made by me to Sallie, that upon her death her ashes will be co-mingled with the ashes of her husband, and distributed at Mayapan, an archaeological site not far from Merida and one of Sallie's favourites. And so I have become, temporarily, the custodian of the ashes which in their handsome looking pressboard containers, I place on the side board in the *sala* at my house. I stand the black framed glyphs drawing in front of the two "urns". On the wall above this new grouping of containers and framed drawing, my own collection of framed this and that, blooms.

Several days later I am passing through the *sala* with the sideboard, when a microscopic flash or a wink or a tic, attracts me over to where I have left the ashes and picture, and I pick up the black framed drawing. I note the pleasing arrangement of line and space in which there are six glyphs with decorative doodles between them. They are, indeed, day glyphs as three of them are immediately recognizable to me from doing the rounds of the Maya calendar. There are three words and a date written in the bottom right corner of the drawing. The words

SALLIE'S GIFT

or names are: *OK, EK, KAAN '98*. The three glyphs I don't recognize immediately have familiar shapes and elements, but I will have to do some checking out and comparison to the glyphs I have sketched from my notes on the Maya days in order to assign a name. In a book borrowed from the Library, I read that glyphs may vary in appearance from region to region and according to the person who has drawn them just as each of us has a distinctive handwriting style.

I stand for a few minutes gazing at the black framed drawing in my hand and I wonder if there could be a message in this for me. This drawing has come my way through a dear friend. It was not of my choosing but I am pleased to have it. Very well, I will take up the invitation, perhaps a challenge, to decipher these messengers and wring out whatever wisdom is to be found in the choice of six glyphs out of a possible twenty. The prospect of doing some "sleuthing" excites me as I gaze at the drawing. What might I conjure from these clues? And so I begin what I came to call, "The Sallie's Gift Project". But that is, as they say, another story.

[35]

MARYETTA ACKENBOM

La Peregrina

"*La Peregrina*" is a song that is always sung here in Yucatan when a person is leaving the area, either permanently or for an extended period. When it is performed appropriately, when someone is going away, it brings tears to the eyes of all who hear it. It is a lovely ballad, one of the first that the visitor or new resident learns to recognize.

"La Peregrina" is the pilgrim, leaving Yucatan. The song was composed in the 1930's, by the Yucatecan composer Ricardo Palmerin, to commemorate the sad departure of an American journalist from Yucatan. Her lover begs her with many florid phrases to stay, to return, or at least, to remember him and Yucatan.

The song has lost popularity because of overuse. A Yucatecan group will unanimously groan if someone requests to hear it—that someone probably being an innocent visitor to the peninsula. But all will weep at the airport, hearing "La Peregrina" as a loved one leaves the area.

I was leaving for an extended period some years ago. A few friends were seeing me off at the airport. I heard a guitar trio tuning up nearby, and soon the unmistakable opening chords of "La Peregrina" came through, loud and clear.

I glanced at my friends, who were grinning like fools, and ducked my head. Flattered, thinking they had arranged the serenade for me, I couldn't stop my tears.

My friends then began to giggle. I was puzzled. Maybe they were tired of hearing the old treasured song, but they should show a rather different emotion since I was leaving them. Was this a joke?

Then I saw a group of several well-dressed men and women gathered nearby. At the edge of the group, the guitar trio. In the middle, the state governor, leaving Merida for Mexico City, appeared embarrassed by the serenade.

My friends burst out laughing. I felt my face turn various shades of red as they gazed at me, eyes full of fun. I had to laugh, too, watching the governor's face, also turning red.

LORNA GAIL DALLIN

To Xocen [show – ken]

To begin, there was something off-footed about the day we were to make the trip to Xocen, all due to me – particularly my expectations. Start with: I thought this day we were going on this expedition, July 18, Monday, was the actual New Year's Day of the Maya calendar. In a quick conversation with Miguel Angel before starting out, I learned that the New Year's Day for this Maya area was July 16, and that the differences in when this New Year's Day is celebrated amongst the various regions where Maya live, are due to the latitude at which the calculation is made. It can range from mid July to early September. Well, that is a range, all right! No wonder I couldn't get an exact answer to my earlier direct question: What Gregorian date corresponds to what date of the Maya calendar? Okay, I get it – and really, it doesn't matter to me (or maybe it does). I just wanted to line up with the prevailing energies, if there are any, around contemplations of the Maya Tzolkin Calendar, an arrangement of days that I have been thinking on in my meditations.

Before we began the trip to Xocen, we had a short explanation from Miguel Angel (a noted Maya scholar and teacher) about the importance of the site to which we would travel, its sacredness, and some idea about how well protected it is – the implication being that you couldn't just wander in off the highway and ask at the village for directions to their sacred site. No, says Miguel Angel, no one would tell you. We also received some instruction on the Maya concepts of sites (and there are several) which they consider to be an **umbilicus**, a navel of the world. One such site lies dormant under the Ball Court of Chich'en Itza. Another is connected to the sacred stone cross at Xocen which we were going to see.

We set out from Merida, and on arrival at the pueblo Miguel Angel found the shaman/guardian of the stones at home. We picked him up and drove to the site. It is a rustic shrine, with a church-like façade – a Maya arch – three tiers surrounding the arch with open-work cinder block, and an entrance into a space that would comfortably accommodate the villagers of Xocen and district, sitting on benches/pews, facing the "altar". The staging for the principle stone which was quite large (3 feet high by less than 2 feet wide?) was commodious and about knee high. Bowls of flowers and plants, along with colourful strings of cut outs and flags, decorated the area. On the altar, there were additional little "closets" (I know there is a name for them but darned if I can remember it) with portraits and photos of old and new villagers, family members and ancestors. These pictures were framed and unframed, large and small, old and new, images and photos. In addition to the pictures of real people there were posters and replicas of Christian saints (read "the Roman Catholic Pantheon") Guadeloupe et al, including a large poster of the face of Jesus Christ – the big, white-faced Jesus with flowing blond locks and beard and blue eyes, fingers up in blessing. I could see no overt signs of the Maya cosmology. They could have, might have been there; an Ixchel perhaps or Kulculkan, or Ahua, but not in plain view. And there was a real crowd of many other things: faux greenery, prints, posters, candles and clouds of copal – sharp, fragrant copal – over all. Lots of crosses, lots of crossing of breasts, crossing with candles, crossing with copal, crossing, bowing ... well, perhaps you get the picture.

We were given candles to light and present, bless, put in holders, take a couple home. When addressing the central large stone cross (the power), we were told by our shaman/guide that we could ask for something – you *can ask the power of the stone to affect something in your life* (I am paraphrasing this instruction, translated by Miguel Angel). Then we were sprinkled with water (several times throughout the ceremony) collected from 7 different *cenotes*. This fact was stressed – water from 7 different *cenotes*, blessed and used to bless us and our visit. The water was sprinkled using a sprig of basil. It truly felt like a blessing when a slight aroma of basil drifted over us. Also with us at this blessing was a Maya family – father, mother, daughter with a young child, and a teen boy all from another pueblo perhaps.

Proceedings drew to a close when the collection basket was passed and the shaman said a few more sincere words to us, translated by Miguel Angel. When the shaman was leading us at the altar, he was speaking Mayan. His addresses to us were in Spanish. After several more turns and an invitation to get up close to the main stone, we were done. We went outside again to our cars, and we drove with the shaman in to town where he took us to the *cenote* which had supplied the village with water for hundreds of years. We saw the shaman/guide back to his home and we returned to Merida.

Now that I have set down the bones of the story of our visit to Xocen, I should look at what bothered me and what blissed me. Believe me; I am sure that my fellow travellers might set down entirely different observations of their impressions of our adventure. It's what makes us human, different points of view. These are my own, personal foibles.

I'll start with the enjoyables; then we can move to the notes that jarred and some that dismayed and the many that pressed my buttons.

I loved the driving there, out in the countryside, someone else behind the wheel, a good driver, me drowsing in the back seat, looking out the window. What is not to ponder in the greenery of a country side in full rainy season lushness, flowers abound. And such a lot of towering clouds in a blue, blue sky, the Big Sky so reminiscent of the Canadian prairie of my youth.

Then there was the quick look we had at Valladolid, a city I have always enjoyed. The town's people have chosen (or so it seemed to me) a lovely colour to be the theme colour of the town – or is it a city? It is a softened Hacienda red, more rose than red. And for me, a glimpse of some of the other remembered haunts. I wondered if the animal carving shoe maker or his apprentices who turned out charming renditions of local animals were still around somewhere. The restaurant in the *Meson de Marques* Hotel where we lunched is now quite upscale; the setting, around the courtyard garden, a Mexican gem. Good food.

The return trip to Merida, provided an excellent opportunity to chat with Miguel Angel and with our driver. To hear Miguel Angel talk about the Maya world he knows so well was a great and enlightening pleasure. To have an opportunity to talk with him about his beliefs was a gift.

I returned to a house of anxious cats. Oscar seemed "run over", walking like an old man. He had probably been wrangling and fighting with the 5 forceful, singularly intent, drooling males all after Miss Siam who was in heat. I scooped her up and took her to the vet to be spayed. This was a sort of metaphorical ending to the day.

Because:
Most of what made me uncomfortable about the day was to be reminded of how father church has bullied its converts. I was reminded of the priests and prelates who jumped on Mother Maya and all but smothered her in their passion to convert. And through this "heat session" lasting a couple of hundred years, the Maya strived to maintain their ceremonies. Perhaps their original intent was to paper over the traditional Maya rites and ritual with enough Roman Catholic bits to put the Church to sleep, leaving the Maya alone to do their own ceremonies in secret.

Well, I don't think that what we saw at Xocen were the real, the hidden rites and rituals. I think we got the mock up, the sanitized, the tourist version.

Or perhaps what we got is just what has evolved over the nearly 500 years since the Euro god came to displace all other gods of the Maya. Maybe I should applaud this co-joined, amalgamated, Roman Catholic/Maya celebration of the sacred stone which came to these Xocen Maya at the time of the first arrival of the Europeans, the dirty hordes rampaging across the land. The Maya called on the gods to give them something, to give them strength, and this stone cross came to them, found by divine revelation in a field near the town. Now it has come to have the power, to be at a navel of the world site.

As amalgamated stories go, this rock has little appeal – not like the Virgin of Guadalupe. Perhaps that is why it seems out of the way, little known. Undoubtedly (according to Miguel Angel) the Maya of Xocen have fostered this obfuscation, keeping their treasure, their messenger from the gods, low key and well guarded.

It is quite likely that I don't have to know, and will not come to know more about this happening place in the *selva* of Yucatan. So I am left with impressions: What did we see when we got there? We saw the rock with a pink drape over it in the way that one sometimes sees crosses in the Yucatan countryside with a *huipil* over them. This covering at Xocen had no embroidery, just a wrap, most of the stone hidden. This putting of the dress over the cross has always reminded me of the sashes and stoles and altar clothes placed over, above and around a well decorated altar in a Christian church. Is this copying? Or is the stone considered in a feminine way that needs a cover?

Crowning my list (or bringing up the rear as the case may be) of what was off-putting: the blue eyed, blond, ringleted, Jesus dominating the left side of the altar area. I just am put off by this person, smirking (and believe me, this poster had a definite smirk to it) over the earnestness of people acting in a sacred manner. We should weep over what has been done in His name.

And what about "touching the stone"? One of the caretakers at the site told D. that no, he couldn't touch it; but then the shaman invited us to do so, pushing aside candles and numerous items on the altar in front of the power stone so we could kneel up closer to touch the large cross with its pink satin "dress". I declined: Why? Because I just did not want to kneel up there and scoot across the altar (on my knees) to touch the stone, then scoot back. What purpose would it serve? On this trip today I did not see myself as a supplicant; there was nothing I wanted to ask of this relic. Did the Maya family touch the stone? They did not. Were they invited to do so? I know not.

So I am left with an uncomfortable feeling about this trip to Xocen, and it is entirely of my own making. I take responsibility for my dis-ease, my un-ease. Mia culpa.

Next, I could write a story about the woman who goes on a sacred journey to a secret site and does not participate in one part of the ceremony. She returns to her home to find chaos amongst the cats – a direct result of her dis-ease and her balking at joining in the mysteries of the day at Xocen.

THERESA DIAZ GRAY

He Lives With Me

As a confirmed optimist, I tend to couch my adventures in the most positive terms. It's not that I forget problems or embarrassing moments; it's that I tend to assign them less importance in the story of my life. However, one incident does stand out.

As the designated Spanish speaker in our household, I am often the one called upon to fill out forms or answer questions. When my husband applied for his INAPAM card, (a senior discount card offered by the Mexican government) I accompanied him. During the application process, an earnest young man read from a list and noted my answers. Things like how many bathrooms do you have? All went well until he wanted to know with whom my husband resided.

"*Con yo* (with me)," I replied brightly. A shocked expression passed over the youngster's features. It suddenly dawned on me that he had heard, "*Coño*", a four letter Spanish word that translates to a four letter English word, also starting with the letter C. Not what you expect to come out of a respectable little old lady's mouth while sitting in a government office.

Fumbling, I sputtered to correct my error, "*Con mi.*"

No, that wasn't it either. Finally, triumphantly, I declared, "*Conmigo.*" I could see the relief on his face as he realized that I didn't have Tourette syndrome. We continued on like nothing had happened.

LORRAINE BAILLIE BOWIE

What I Meant to Say

If you refer to your neighbor as a horse, say you are horny, and announce your pregnancy, most Yucatecans know you meant to say the word gentleman, you find the weather stifling, and you are not pregnant, only embarrassed. We foreign speakers fight to piece together the scraps and snippets of what we think we know into a mosaic we hope will result in a congenial conversation. However, on occasion, even the most practiced listener struggles to decipher what we meant to say. One of the many challenges facing even the most discriminating Yucatecan is that we novice speakers generate three levels of language, only one of which is verbalized. First, is what we wish we could say, second, what we thought we said, and third, what we said.

After a delicious and filling feast at a downtown Merida restaurant, my husband Roger applied his point-at-the-picture style of ordering dessert. Not one to bow to the easy, I challenged my sparse vocabulary to order my dessert. I wanted to say, "The dinner was lovely, but I'm afraid I didn't leave much room, so I'll just have a little slice, a sliver really, of chocolate cake."

The chances of turning these thoughts into a coherent request were as slim as winning an argument with a four-year-old. I stared at the pattern of parrots on the tablecloth, as if they would spit out the words I needed. When the colorful birds ignored me, I flung my few words together and thought I said, "Give me a little cake please."

The server, with a bandolier crisscrossed across his chest and a tourist style sombrero, returned with a red and green hand-woven basket with a container each of Tums, Pepto-Bismol, and Aspirin. I had no words to express my surprise and confusion. Roger reminded me that his point and order skills had yielded him a generous serving of mango crisp with vanilla ice cream while the waiter presented me with an assortment of medications.

In unreserved confusion, I looked around the room, searching for a solution to a problem for which I had no language to identify. A fellow North American diner at the table to my left, wearing shorts and espadrilles, placed her frozen margarita on the tail of a silent tablecloth parrot and executed a much-appreciated language intervention. According to her, what I said was, "Give me a pill, please." She explained that when I held my hand over my stomach to show that I was full and asked for a pill, the waiter thought I was ill. To the worried waiter, she clarified that I was trying to order the cake (*pastel*) and not a pill (*pastilla*.) In typical Yucatecan style of not wanting to embarrass a foreign speaker, the waiter asked if I preferred chocolate or *tres leche* pills.

WHAT I MEANT TO SAY

While I received offers of medicine instead of dessert, my friend, let's call her Mary, suffered from a medical problem compounded by a language blunder. Mary, a warm, friendly woman with a broad, toothy grin and a talent for painting and gardening, faced four days of boring bed rest following hip surgery. She had every confidence in the expertise of the nursing staff but worried about her ability to communicate should she need something. Until now, her urinary catheter permitted her to avoid asking for a particular piece of hospital equipment. Following a bedtime laxative, she awoke early the next morning with an urgent request. Mary attacked the call button as if she knew the answer on Jeopardy, squeezed her butt cheeks together, stared at the doorway, and awaited the nurse's arrival.

The sound of rustling cotton preceded a plump nurse who soon filled the doorway with her generous smile and offers of assistance. Mary wished to say, "If you are sure that I am not allowed to walk to the bathroom, I'll need the bedpan, please. I think it's in the bathroom. Please hurry as I took a laxative last night."

Recognizing the futility of translating what she wanted to say while holding back the products of last night's cathartic, Mary thought she said, "Please, bring my bedpan (*cuña*) from the bathroom. Hurry!"

In dismay, Mary watched the nurse turn and dart from the room, leaving the doorway barren, but only for a moment. The nurse returned with an English speaking doctor who, even faster than Mary's racing heartbeat, assessed the situation and sped the bedpan to her side. Later, when visiting with her own doctor, who also spoke excellent English, Mary found that what she said was, "Give me my ass (*culo*) and hurry!" Mary blushed and said that she was pregnant. Her doctor's eyes twinkled; she knew Mary was only embarrassed.

Lena, newly arrived from Canada and wearing sensible Canadian sandals, also had a request, although less urgent than Mary's need for a bedpan. Lena heard that select seamstresses in both Merida and the beach communities craft clothes by copying an existing garment. I never had clothing copied, but I knew of an alteration shop on *Circuito Colonias* that I thought might also copy clothes. I gave Lena the directions. When Lena addressed the teenaged clerk sporting a neon-orange headband and fuchsia mascara, she wanted to say, "I understand that some seamstresses fabricate clothes from looking at an article of clothing. If you provide this service, I have two sundresses I would like copied." Powerless to execute her lengthy request, but smug in her ability to shorten her message, she thought she said, "Can you sew (*coser*) a copy of my clothes?"

The actual question landing on unsuspecting ears was, "Can you cook (*cocinar*) my clothes?" The clerk blinked her fuchsia eyelashes and rushed her zebra-striped manicured fingers to her mouth. Lena was sure she had unleashed a language faux pas that hung in the air, like a jaguar about to pounce on his prey. The clerk sidestepped the jaguar and beckoned a worker from one of the six sewing machines to help with Lena's request.

After a brief consultation, the two directed Lena to the dry cleaners across the street. No doubt they decided dry cleaning was the closest they could think of for cooking clothes. At the dry cleaners, Lena again asked to have her clothes cooked. Fortunately, for Lena, the young clerk summoned an older woman, with large hands scarred from the pressing table, who spoke enough English to explain the difference between the verbs to cook and to sew.

WHAT I MEANT TO SAY

Grocery shopping, even more than cooking clothes, is ripe for embarrassing miscommunications for the newcomer, the upside being an occasional humorous interlude for those trying to make sense of the request. The cheese table at Mega flaunted an attractive assortment of aromatic cheeses, Longhorn, Colby, Monterey Jack, and even the hard to find Cheddar. Roger enjoyed seeing the rare cheeses side by side with the abundant local cheese, Manchego. The display reminded him of his neighborhood in El Centro, a few happy-to-be-here foreigners living side by side with welcoming and tolerant Meridians. Unable to find the cheese he needed for his recipe, he caught the eye of an employee whose name tag introduced her as Rosita. When Rosita saw a shock of white hair framing a weathered complexion void of color and driven by inquiring blue eyes, she knew a language disaster was imminent. Too late to escape his question, she forced a smile and asked how she could help.

Roger wanted to say, "I'm looking for goat cheese, herb encrusted if you have it. If not, plain or garlic will be okay."

Expressing the term herb encrusted surpassed Roger's language skills, so he put thumbs and forefingers together to simulate a role of cheese and thought he said, "Goat cheese (*cabra*) please."

Rosita flinched, took a step backward and splayed her hands in front of her as if to ward off a wild animal. Roger, sure his word for goat was correct, decided the problem was his elocution. He repeated the word goat at least five times to afford the listener plenty of opportunities to process his faulty pronunciation.

"Cobra cheese, please." That's right; he said cobra, that hooded snake that can reach up to eighteen feet in length.

[53]

Rosita indicated they did not sell snake cheese, but Roger insisted that they did. His thumb and forefinger imitation of a role of cheese looked exactly like a snake to Rosita, especially since he continued to repeat, "Cobra cheese, I know you have it."

An amused crowd made way for Senor Gomez, an affable manager with an easy smile and a buzz haircut. He listened to Roger's request and led him to a nearby display groaning with a hefty assortment of flavors and brands of goat cheese. "Aha," said Roger, thinking, "Finally someone who understands me." The manager walked away chuckling; this was not his first rodeo.

∞

The people of Yucatan encourage and praise us for our small successes in speaking their language, but also, from asses to snake cheese, strive never to let us suffer embarrassment for our mistakes. The occasional private chuckle is a well-deserved reward for their patient spirits and generous hearts.

CHERIE PITTILLO

A Sustainable Tradition

When my bi-lingual friends, Sigmund and Sela told me about a family that protected their hundred-year old forest in the Yucatan, I urged them to introduce me to learn how any forest could survive where few trees escaped the slash and burn methods of the Maya. Since most of the Yucatan state's forests have been clear-cut, I am fascinated about this family.

Their decades-old secrets of their location and their names will be safe with me, but I can share the gist of what they do. I will call them the Che' family, the Mayan name for "wood". Juan, their son/grandson, is our guide to discover this sustainable tradition.

My friends and I drive to a remote Maya jungle where this multi-generational family preserves this old growth forest, all 250 acres (100 hectares), the source for their livelihood of basketry. Those basket weaving vines they require only live in an old growth forest. I worked with a sustainable forest project in the US, but this is the easiest sustainable forest project I've ever known.

After about a three hour drive, we leave the comfort of a paved road to drive down a rocky road. Beside it, three silvery strands of barbed wire slice through where another old growth forest had lived for more than 100 years. I stare at the fence and wonder how this space looked before the long-lived trees fell at the strong hands of a machete-wielding *campesino* (rural person).

A scrubby, arid mess, not cultivated for several years, borders the road. Brown and black weed skeletons stand guard over what was, and reach out to the car beyond the barbed wire with barbs of their own.

On the other side of the road a forest grows, each young tree competing for which can be the quickest to claim the nutrients from the shallow soil. It's survival of the fittest for these invasive shrubs and trees that sprout multiple trunks in this race to survive. They are not so much a forest as a tangled chaos of small, many-stemmed shrubs and trees.

After twenty minutes, I don't relish this slow drive on a long road as potholes seem hungry to eat the car. Limbs screech as they scratch the car as if to escape their imposed prison.

Along the way, I stop the car for Sela to leave an offering at a foot high wooden cross braced upright on a large rock sitting atop a vine-covered boulder. On the crosspiece is the name of the Maya village, my destination. In front of the cross my friend delicately drops a small stone which joins other pebbles there. That tiny rock is to give us safe travel to the village.

As we proceed for another fifteen minutes, a shock of low growing bright green grass in a 50 x 50 foot spot of land adjacent to the road contrasts with the tiny-trunked trees and the black and gray of the surroundings. That patch of grass provides livestock food and seems to be the only plants maintained along this road.

Occasionally a trail or a small dirt road cuts off to the left, but most of the left side is fenced in with scattered saw palmettos and those weeds. I didn't see any remnants of any corn stalks that would have grown at one time in this abandoned *milpa* (cornfield*)*. Now I see inside the fence where a campesino exposes mounds of rocky limestone as he clears the land for a new milpa with a machete, again.

Finally we approach the tiny village and we see a one-room, concrete block school for first to sixth grades (*primaria*), a concrete house under a few large trees, a bare concrete slab, and in the distance, a *nah (*Maya wooden house with a thatched palm roof). I smell smoke. I make a 90 degree turn and enter coolness as we arrive at the Che' homes.

Immediately on my right is their concrete house. We are greeted by Juan, our guide, who escorts us to a nah, the first home of his parents. On the way, we pass another nah that is the current kitchen for the families. Chickens scratch at the rocky ground and two cats hang around the kitchen entry. Purple flowers adorn the walkway. In front of the kitchen, a thatched roof shelter with no walls contains a huge caldron where a fire roars. On a nearby hillside I see Juan's home, for him, his wife and three daughters.

Juan uses a forked stick to fish two coils of vines out of the boiling, hot water-containing caldron. He undoes the first coil and straightens about thirty vines of various lengths to run along the ground into the confines of his parents first home. Sticks supporting the thatched roof remind me of the forest I glimpsed upon our arrival. Shafts of light filter through a gap in the roof and the walls.

Inside, Juan, his parents, wife, sister, my friends, and I begin to strip the wet outer bark from each vine by hand. The heated water enables that protective coating to loosen. It feels thick and rough but once removed, the pale yellow vine is smooth except at each joint. Most vines in this coil are about 25 feet long. After bark removal, each strand becomes a circle again as we gather it into another coil and hand it to Juan.

I look at all of us sitting in a circle just like the vine was a few minutes ago. But I also think how this circle of family binds together in the livelihood of basketry, and also as a family whose members support each other.

Juan, his wife, and father wear modern clothing as they sit on small wooden stools or wooden blocks to work the vines. Both his mom and his sister wear *huipiles* (traditional white dress with hand-embroidered designs). His sixty-nine year old mom sits in a short metal chair as she works.

Although children start removing the bark off the vines at seven or eight years of age, they are not permitted to cut the vines in the forest for the baskets. Only five men and Juan's sister decide which vines to cut and where. As a seven year old, Juan began to strip the vine bark and didn't make his first basket until he was 22. Now he is 32. He smiles with pride as he states his daughters are interested in the family business, and the oldest, at 12 years, designs different styles.

Juan's father cuts off the thicker joints with a butcher knife, and everyone else begins to make baskets. Depending on the size to be made, Juan takes a flimsy measuring tape to measure and cut the first piece, which serves as a guide to cut the rest of each vine. When I was twenty-two, I learned to make baskets from oak strips in a similar process.

Once Juan gathers seven pieces, he quickly weaves them. He uses his bare feet to hold down the bottom of the basket.

A SUSTAINABLE TRADITION

I'd never seen anything like that. He starts with four strands running in front of his feet with three strands running between his legs. Then he begins coiling one vine around those seven strands for the basket bottom.

With that foot-hold, strand after strand continues to be inserted and vine ends are sharpened with small knives to make points for easy insertion into this circular creation. His mother and wife repeat the same process with their feet while his father continues to cut off those rough vine joints.

When I look around the hut, I see a hammock, lifted up and attached to a ceiling joist. Several sizes of vine globes hang from the ceiling and vary from five inch to twenty inch spheres. Those globes do not require foot holding to make them. I thought how those light, airy, loosely woven, see-through balls reminded me of the inter-connectedness of this family as well as how the earth is also intertwined with its natural resources and people.

When the basket increases from a few strands to a larger size, the feet don't hold down the basket, which is completed by hand. In twelve minutes Juan's mom creates a 10 x 6 x 8 inch basket. She is the *maestra*, who brought this tradition to this family from her mother and her mother's mother, on into past ages.

In 1960, at 15, she met her future husband in her village as they were both *jarana* (traditional dance after colonization) dancers. They were married when he was 19 and she was 18. Prior to the marriage, Juan's father bought the 250 acres from his father. When he brought his new wife to see their new homeland, she saw the vines in the old forest and shared her multi-generational basketry skills with her husband.

Juan's uncle, his father's brother, also bought 250 acres of land, but he cleared it to be leased for agriculture. Typically

[59]

this is the most common use of wooded land due to traditions of slash and burn techniques to clear the land to grow crops. These methods, also known as swidden, date back to the Maya to 2500 BC.

Then the time comes for Sigmund, Sela and me to enter the old growth forest with Juan in the lead. As we follow a path, immediately a tall banana grove greets us. At twenty-five feet tall, I think this grove has the healthiest, tallest banana trees I'd ever seen. A young forest, owned by his uncle, borders us as we walk down a road and I see no vines.

And then we enter the preserved old growth forest.

An indeterminate, subtle sweet smell fills my nostrils. For a few minutes we stay on the trail and then Juan meanders off-trail through the forest. As he walks, he shows us several species of vines…not in trees but on top of the ground. How quickly he spots them and how easily they blend into the forest floor. He picks one up with his *koa* (curved knife), cuts it and states, "This one is not good for baskets. See how the center is hollow?"

To me the exterior looks just like the other vines. How did he know this one was different?

I remark, "I thought the vines would grow up or around the trees."

"Most of the vines we use run along the ground. The longest runs 60-88 feet (20-25 meters); the shortest, a rare solid deep scarlet one, extends only 33 feet (10 meters)."

We continue to wend our way through the forest; I ask about the tree species or other plants. Juan carefully explains the Mayan name, how the plants are used medicinally or for livestock or for food. His knowledge reminds me of a wizened professor. Occasionally vines have a woody base and grow up the tree but Juan says the tree canopy and leaf litter are requirements for the vines to grow healthily along the ground.

A SUSTAINABLE TRADITION

I couldn't believe the incredible, crisscross network below my feet and thought how many people who are used to manicured lawns would see this maze of green and gray as a jumbled disarray. Limbs, vines, and some dead trees were scattered throughout this forest floor. How happy Sigmund and Sela were to experience the forest off the well-traveled path. Prior to this visit, they had only been on specific trails for about thirty minutes although they've known this family for more than fifteen years.

Although we didn't see the largest tree Juan knows of, he said it would take three men to reach around its base. That tree is the ceiba, *yax che* in Mayan, the sacred tree of the Maya. This forest is 80 – 100 years old and Juan's grandfather was the one who protected it.

I ask to be left alone for a few minutes for contemplation and to experience this forest by myself. I wanted to feel how the forest would reveal itself when I simply stood still.

One tree rubs its bark against another in a squeaky song. I hear a gentle breeze from the treetops and then the fast zoom of a flying insect. I watch small insects fly low to the ground. When I look at tree trunks, I see a patchwork of bark with lichens from brown to gold to silver, and many shades of green.

A *mariposa* (butterfly) with long black forewings with a brush stroke of bright red comes near me. I see vines on the ground and those reaching to wind around trees. Then several more mariposas arrive. One perches on a limb and it looks like green stained glass outlined in tan. Another, the cracker, with colors of gray, splotchy tree bark, lands on a nearby tree with its head pointed down and outstretched wings to blend into the bark. A large white mariposa flippy-flops through the forest. I see seven species in colors from yellow to white to brown with blue. Their sizes and flight patterns vary like the trees, large to small, high to low.

The breeze reaches my face to cool it, although I hadn't felt hot. A brown lichen on a tree had the shape of a bear. But no bears live in these woods. Juan said deer were the largest animals he's seen in this forest.

I rejoin Juan and my friends reluctantly.

We return to a road, then a path, and come upon two wooden crosses, one on each side of our trail. The crosses serve as land boundary markers. Villagers know that bad winds exist in the forest. They ask a shaman to hold a traditional ceremony to protect the land, crops, people, and animals. While the shaman walks around the perimeter, he burns chilies, beetles, and scatters feathers from a soon-to-be-sacrificed chicken. He gives power to the crosses which lasts about 8-10 years. Also, he plants a different vine that doesn't grow in this forest at each cross but somehow it thrives.

In a few years, if dogs become lost and chickens die, then the villagers ask for the shaman to return. If not, people get headaches, fevers, vomit or may die. It's important for the shaman to return because the bad winds can now cause hardship on animals and people in the village.

When we return to Juan's grandparents' home, I ask how old is their low-roofed concrete house complete with a small TV satellite dish. He said the house was 18 years old but when it's hot, they stay in the Maya huts due to the coolness created by the high-rise, thatched palm roofs. During the winter or a bad storm, they live in the concrete house because it's warmer and safer in bad weather.

Next, Juan invites me to visit the family milpa and I readily accept. Although I would love to hike there, due to time constraints–it's now 2 pm–we drive out the entry rocky road to another road to then drive to the milpa, a 2.5 acre plot. Enclosed by a barbed wire fence, this hilly land is covered in dead weeds and patches of wild grasses. Juan says the deer come out at night to graze. I ask if they hunt the game.

Juan remarks, "Our family doesn't hunt. We don't own a gun and we don't allow any hunting on our land." I'm astonished. In many villages I typically see men on bicycles with their rifles or shotguns strapped across their backs. Instead of wild game, the Che' family eats their own chickens, turkeys, ducks, and pigs.

Again, Juan leads the way past this milpa as we enter into a younger forest. It is their wood source for fuel, cooking, and heating that cauldron. I linger behind to compare this young forest (*monte*) with the old growth forest (*monte alta*, tall forest). This one is not as tall and the tree trunks are thinner.

Suddenly he announces, "We are at the battlefield."

As I arrive at the forest edge, I realize what an apt description "battlefield" is. It looked like an explosion killed all the trees. Recently felled trees litter the ground. Stumps dot the landscape. This area will be their second milpa.

I ask, "Why couldn't some of the trees be saved for shade?"

"If we leave a tree, birds will sit in the tree, watch us plant our seeds, and then steal the seeds. If we leave a tree for shade, and then burn this field, it could harm the tree and then it could fall on us as we work."

Next we approach a 10 foot wide circle of sticks made into a pyramid, which will become charcoal. Many layers of former tree trunks and limbs, each about one yard long, are piled on top of each other. Each one leans at a 75 degree angle to make this structure about six feet high. The center has the driest wood. I have never seen a wooden pyramid, only the Maya stonework of their ancient pyramids.

Covered in leaves and small brush, the mound is topped with dirt. One stick, which runs along the ground in the middle of the wood pile, is pulled out. Carved on one end it is covered with a diesel laden cloth, then lit with a fire. This gigantic match stick is reinserted into the stacked wood. More dirt is added around and on top of the pyramid to keep the fire burning slowly for five to eight days. Each pyramid produces 80 to 100 waist-high bags of charcoal.

I remark, "I thought with slash and burn techniques that all the trees were cut and then everything was set on fire. Land is cleared and burned so that crops can be planted. Then after a few years, the soil is infertile and another forest is cleared again."

"Most farmers do just clear cut and then burn. They never use the trees. But we use what nature has given us, so we recycle the trees by making charcoal. We will do this little by little. Plus we use all sizes. It requires more work and takes more time, but we reuse what the land gives us," Juan explains.

"Have you ever had a fire burn any forest on your property?"

"No. We use buffers around our land. We camp out around our property during the burning season and we stay here when we make the charcoal to monitor the fire."

Now I ask, "So how many milpas will you make in this young forest? Won't you keep clearing more land?"

"No, we will have only these two milpas."

"But how can you? Doesn't the soil become infertile? I know the ashes add some soil nutrition, but eventually that is used up."

"No, because we don't use pesticides and we can reuse the land many years."

A SUSTAINABLE TRADITION

Juan explains about their crops of corn, two kinds of squash, pumpkin, jicama, sweet potatoes, and beans. Squash rinds are boiled to feed the pigs. The family doesn't waste anything.

Before the ears of corn are harvested, the top half of the corn stalks are bent down to hide the ripening corn from birds and to give it shade. Beans grow up the corn stalks for support and the squash serve as a groundcover to reduce weeds. He showed two kinds of squash; one with large seeds and one with small seeds, used as soup squash. Sela called the corns, beans, and squash, "the trinity". In the US, Native Americans call them the three sisters.

I am dumbfounded by what I've learned about this family and their lifestyle. How can this young man and his family go against what I thought was Maya traditions such as the repetitive slash and burn techniques of clearing land and the killing game for food? Later I talk with an archaeologist who explained the Maya had many traditions including working in harmony with the land. She even mentioned that some used specific insects to protect their crops.

I realized the Che' family wasn't going against their culture. I only knew about the generalized traditions. I'm humbled to have met this family and heard their story. I also realize how easy it is to assume and to be wrong.

I had one last question when we returned to the family compound, I asked, "What lessons have you learned about sustainability, Juan?"

"My grandfather said to take care of the land and the land will give to you. He also said to harvest the basket weaving vines only from the old growth forest. The milpa is on part of the land not in the old growth. He built the first house here in 1910 and the community grew from that."

"I learned from my father's example, too. I saw that my father

[65]

didn't cut down the trees and the materials that came from the forest would sustain us. I am teaching my daughters that we can live by preserving our culture."

Although my visit lasted only six hours, I learned this was more than a sustainable old growth forest project. Now I understood how life and culture are maintained generation after generation.

GWEN LANE

Yucatan Sol

Yucatan Sol warms my soul. Flaring gases, twirling world.
Overtakes the grip of dark, with rays of wisdom, knowledge and hope.
Zenith Sol burns its cross above the hours.
Cooling clouds spread diamond sparkles,
Until Luna chases Sol through the west gate,
Dominates the night and shines with promise for my soul tomorrow.
Yucatan Sol rests my soul.

Yucatan Sol soothes my soul. Calm, nature, endures.
Awakening birds call companions and fly to flirt.
Blowing breezes, blossoms bestow.
Iguanas silently sunning in the peace of the heat, listen to the sound of the ages.
Taste buds ignite when touched by Yucatan delights,
Panuchos, Poc Chuc, Pibil, Pastor, Soups, Salbutes, Sandwichon and more.
Yucatan Sol refreshes my soul.

Yucatan Sol sweetens my soul with treasures;

UNIQUELY YUCATAN

Sun of gold, rain of diamonds, moon of silver, jungles of emerald.
Flowers brighter than rubies nourish sweet amber honey.
Turquoise waves temper thirst.
Bright bird songs erupt into sapphire sky filled with clouds of ivory and pearl.
A place where heaven and nature wed;
Yucatan Sol graces my soul.

MARYETTA ACKENBOM

The Burning Season

The late afternoon sun hung like a giant red-orange symbol of the end of creation. Below it, shades of mauve and lavender faded into the dark line of the horizon. I turned from packing my small suitcase to speak to my friend, Luisa.

"The burning season is really upon us. Look at that sun!"

She joined me at the window. "We always have these incredible sunsets in the spring. The farmers burn their fields before they do their planting."

"Yes, I remember. The smoke clouds the atmosphere and gives the sun that unreal color." I had seen the burning season sun for the first time last year.

We stood and watched the engorged sun as it began to disappear in the West.

I turned toward Luisa. "Let's go find something to eat. Do you want to go into town?"

"No, let's eat here at the hotel. I'm tired, and I'm afraid we'll run into some of the fishermen."

Driving from Merida, Mexico, where we both worked at the U.S. Consulate in the early 1970s, we had arrived the evening before on Isla Mujeres, a small fishing and tourist island off the Caribbean coast of Yucatan. We spent the day negotiating with local customs and police officials, trying to obtain the release of two U.S. fishing boats. Thanks to the persuasive ability of Luisa, the Consulate's specialist in dealing with problems of U.S. citizens, we managed to obtain a solid "maybe" from the Isla Mujeres officials. They told us that without any doubt, the boats had been caught fishing within Mexican territorial waters and were subject to confiscation. Payment of hefty fines would probably get the boats released to their captains, who followed us around all day long and raised all kinds of heck by telephone with the Consulate in Merida, 200 miles away, and the U.S. Embassy in Mexico City, 1,200 miles away.

Luisa and I had done our part and planned to leave in the morning to take the ferry back to the mainland, pick up my car where we left it yesterday with an eager young parking attendant, and drive back to Merida.

We dined on an excellent fresh snapper. When we finished eating we went out to look at the moonlit water one last time.

"It's a shame we have to go back so soon," I said, watching the moonbeams playing on the waves. "I could really use a few days on the beach. The Consul should rearrange his schedule so he could cover for us."

"You're kidding! He wouldn't do that. Besides, he's had his vacation trip planned for several weeks. You just have to admit we're indispensable."

I laughed. "Sure we are. All the Consul did was remind us of those kidnappings on the highways. Let's get some rest so we can start early tomorrow and take our time on the road."

The ferry ride back to the mainland in the morning was routinely gorgeous. The colors of the water and the beaches of the Caribbean islands off the coast of Yucatan are unique in the world. The combination of aqua, purple and infinitely deep blue water with the white sand of the beaches and the varied green of the island flora spread before our eyes like the tail of an immense peacock.

We picked up the car, tipped the youngster who had guarded it from damage, and started driving west toward Merida.

The roads were always a little frightening because at any moment people and their animals, as well as wild animals, could step out into the right-of-way. Going through the small towns, we always slowed to a crawl. We stayed constantly alert to changing conditions. Ours was the only car on the narrow road.

We spent two hours companionably talking about what had happened and planning a subsequent trip. Maybe we could rent a boat next time and go fishing. And we would definitely bring our snorkeling gear.

Looking ahead, I saw a black smudge on the horizon. I pointed it out to Luisa, who was driving.

"It must be the burning," she said.

A small shiver went down my spine. "That's why no cars are coming this way. Would the burning be that close to the road? Or is that an illusion?"

"The fires do get out of control, but I think that's farther away than it looks."

The ugly black cloud crept closer as we continued. Then, without being aware of when it happened, we were surrounded by thick smoke.

Luisa turned on the headlights. We could not see the road.

"Hey," I said. "We didn't ask for this. What do we do now?"

"I think we just have to creep along. If we stop we could be run over by another car."

"Or the fire could overtake us!"

"That, too."

We crept. The air conditioner helped, but it didn't close out all of the smoke. Soon we became uncomfortable. Flashes of flame shot up at the sides of the road. I could barely make out darker billows of smoke where brush burned in roadside fields. There was no sign of life anywhere, except for the life of the monstrous clouds of smoke and tongues of flame. Fifteen minutes passed.

I worried about the car. Was the road too hot, would the tires melt? Would the smoke choke off the motor? What if we ran off the road? We crept.

Suddenly the smoke cleared as quickly as it had descended upon us.

Luisa stopped the car. We were both shaking. "Would you mind driving for a while?" she asked.

"Sure, soon as I catch my breath." My heart raced as I changed places with her.

I started up quickly and tried to make time on the blacktop road. In the distance ahead of us I could see another black smudge. The road was ominously empty of life.

Within five minutes smoke again engulfed us. Sparks flew against the windshield. My knuckles tightened on the wheel as I slowed the car down. Again we crept.

For another ten minutes we continued our scary trek. I imagined headlines in the local press, "Consular Officers Burned in Cornfield. Martyred While Rescuing Fishing Boats." Then, finally, the smoke began to thin, and we saw small groups of men along the roadside who could have been either setting the fire or tending it. The men straightened up from their work and stared at us as we passed. A few lifted their hands in a tentative salute.

I began to breath normally again. "Luisa, I think we're alive."

I heard the clicking of her rosary. "Amen."

We waved at the groups gathered along the roadside.

The smoke became thinner and thinner, and we opened the windows wide, leaving the air conditioner on full blast. We were grinning like fools.

We raced for home, hoping to avoid any replay of our adventure.

An anxious consulate staff greeted us when we arrived. The Consul threw up his hands and shouted, "Where have you been? We've called the police, the highway patrols, everyone we could think of on Isla Mujeres! We thought you'd been kidnapped. Don't you remember that we've had threats about political kidnappings?"

We did not expect this. What had we done to deserve a scolding? We could have been incinerated!

I lashed back at the boss: "Hey, we came back as fast as we could. You know, we almost got burned up on the road. Didn't we call you?" I thought for a moment. "Oh, I guess we forgot to call last night. But I didn't think you'd be this upset. It was only one day."

The Consul was not appeased. He turned his back and went into his office, to call off the police and notify the Embassy that the truants had turned up. No one wanted to hear about our adventures on the road. The staff went back to work, ignoring us. They let us know later that we had been the cause of much ranting on the part of the Consul, and indeed, we had caused quite a bit of extra work for them. Luisa and I sat at our desks mulling over the piles of work that had appeared during our absence. At closing time we went to my house and commiserated over a couple of stiff drinks.

"Luisa," I said, "we are not indispensable. No one even cares."

"Yes they do. They called the police. They simply don't care about the same things we do. We have the memories of the trip and the beautiful island to keep forever. The burning on the road—that will just spice up the memories."

She was right. I have seen the huge red burning-season sun a number of times since our escape from the fires. Always in the back of my mind is the realization that if the cruelly inefficient slash-and-burn agricultural system were replaced by more modern technology, the dramatic sky it caused would never again appear. And the unreal quality of the magnified sun also reminds me that closer to earth, the effects of those fires can also be unbearably dramatic.

CHERIE PITTILLO

Creature of Shadow and Sun: Snowy Egret

Creature of shadow and sun
Of light and dark
Question mark neck
Pointed with plumes
Sunrise golden lores
Coordinate with spindly feet
Yellow-seamed, black stockings
Stalking on quartet of stilet-toes
Ruffling fluff of feathers
Creating lift with wings of lace
For a liquid dance of freedom

First published in The Yucatan Times, Backyard Birding in Merida, Yucatan and Beyond

CHERIE PITTILLO

Artist's Palette

Turquoise-browed Motmot

Artist's palette
Of Yucatan seasons
Verdant from rain
Green-mixed russet from dry
Amber of sunsets
Turquoise of Caribbean
Deep scarlet of Flor de Mayo
Maya blue of cenotes
Blackness of starless night

Sam Ervin's eyebrows
Amy Winehouse-lined eyes
Electric blue-lined goatee
Tennis racket-tipped tail

UNIQUELY YUCATAN

Utility line enhancer
Concrete wall lounger
Fence wire sitter
Dead tree topper

Complete artist's brush
In morning fog

First published in The Yucatan Times, Backyard Birding in Merida, Yucatan and Beyond

LORNA GAIL DALLIN

The Queen of Mexico...
The Queen of Heaven

We each of us come to our passions in different ways. My abiding interest in Our Lady of Guadalupe came slowly. In the acclimatization to my Mexican environment, I was sure that there was nothing of interest to me in the religious life of Mexico, nothing that could illuminate aspects of my adopted country. Indeed, if my own personal religious climate was of no interest to me (I was actively shedding all traces of it) there could be nothing in Mexico's very Catholic world that would speak to me. And so I was mostly unaware of and unmoved by the glory of *La Guadalupana* until a writer by the name of Carla Zarebska came on my scene. My interest in the Virgin of Guadalupe changed because of (not surprisingly) a book.

Images of the Virgin first entered my consciousness in the late 1980s while living on Isla Mujeres. *La Isla* is not known to be a hotbed of religious fervor, but is a fairly stable Mexican fishing community which celebrated the Virgin's Day of December 12th with processions through the sandy streets to the port where the fisher folk had a special ceremony involving the Virgin and the blessing of the fleet. The principal Catholic Church on the island, perched beside the Main Square, had a shrine to Guadalupe. On one side of the church was a basketball court and on the other side, snuggled into a slight rise, was a substantial shrine which we in our witty-ness irreverently nicknamed "Our Lady of Las Vegas". What we saw was a female figure surrounded by chase lights, spotlights, votive candles and of course, bouquets of plastic flowers in tin can vases. This spot was a perfect landmark for an assignation, or you could make it a walk destination. After a stroll around the plaza, we would "visit" the shrine to see what new treasures had been left for the Lady. What did we know, what did we care about the devotion shown at this place. A cynic might suggest that this Queen was "invented" by the Catholic Church to bring the heathen into the fold and make the new religion more palatable to *los indios*. Plunder, rape, subdue; what wit bent on that agenda could conceive of the Virgin of Guadalupe. It was easy to dismiss her.

Some years later in another Mexican setting, this time in Merida, along came Carla with her stupendous book about the Virgin of Guadalupe which gave us a whole big picture of this Queen of Mexico. In 2004, as she promoted her book, Carla brought us an understandable setting for *Nuestra Señora*. In photos, text, and poems with writings from Spanish Officials and Church Fathers of the day, this miraculous story unfolds. Carla loved to speak about the subject she had researched so thoroughly and she entertained us with talks about Our Lady. Of course I started looking for more books and more authors which brought on an avalanche of information and speculation. I was hooked. I needed to write this story in my own words in order to capture it for myself. And this is the story I found.

THE QUEEN OF MEXICO

In most of Mexico, the Christmas Season begins around the end of November. As the days of *Hanal Pixan* wind down, it is time to close the portal between the worlds of the quick and the dead which has been open and very accessible during all of November. Yucatecans now look forward to a time in the not too distant future when the days will begin to get longer. And into this period of waiting for the winter solstice, comes the celebration of the Virgin of Guadalupe; the Queen of Mexico, the Queen of Heaven.

The story of this miraculous manifestation begins in 1531, winter. To set the scene; it is less than a dozen years since Cortes landed on the shores of Veracruz. The original inhabitants of the country have been completely defeated. The Aztec/Mexica way of life is in ruins. The years after the conquest have been indescribably painful for the Indian survivors and they have come to believe that their gods have truly abandoned them. How was it possible that they, who had lived in constant adoration and work toward the gods (male and female,) should be suffering this unimaginable end of their world?

It is said that the great god, Quetzalcoatl, has fled promising to return at a later date. Adios, see you later. There are no longer sacrifices to the sun and yet it continues to rise each morning. The statues and relics of the gods and goddesses of the Aztec/Mexica are smashed, their places of worship razed. And from the rubble comes another city with bizarre new buildings and priests who expound a strange idea about a single god, a god remote and terrible. The Mexica see no images of the new god and yet they are invited, even ordered to join his worship. Why go on living if the familiar gods have forgotten them?

The chief lords of the Aztec/Mexica people as well as their governors and officials have been executed; huge pyres burned with the codices that held Indian history and traditions. Terrible epidemics and floods have swept the land and laid waste to the people. And now, the first mixed race children, products of the rape of Indian women, were considered less than human and many abandoned or killed; Indian children were separated from their parents and raised by the church until adulthood when they were considered converted and returned to their families who knew them not. Some religious conversions took place willingly, or more often, forcibly. The indigenous nutrition has been drastically altered by the foods of the conquerors and to add more injury, the Aztec/Mexican men consume large quantities of alcohol given to them by the Spaniards. Drunkenness became a way of life.

In this chaotic country of conquest, the Indians became objects of continued abuse and misunderstanding. Their character and their personality, once haughty and proud, became withdrawn, suspicious of anything relating to the "white world", now they are shy, their gaze fixed on the ground as they try to get by in this new life, unnoticed by the overlords. All was changed, changed utterly and not for the better.

And into this desolate scene on or about 12th, December, 1531, walks Juan Diego, an Aztec convert to Christianity. He is crossing Tepeyac hill, at dawn, a hill very near the new city of Mexico. He hears birds singing at the top of the hill. The music is exquisite, ethereal. And out of the mists comes the figure of a young woman walking towards him. She stops and smiles at him. Juan Diego stands before her, filled with admiration. Her dress shines like the sun, it seems to shimmer and the rock, the crag on which she comes to stand, seems to throw rays of light. Her radiance is gem-like ... everything most beautiful.

Juan prostrates himself before the vision. The young woman smiles on him and speaks. She speaks to him in Nahuatl, his own native dialect and asks him to do something for her, he will be rewarded, she says. *She wants to show her compassionate self to those who seek her comfort*, and to that end she desires a sacred home to be built on this hill. "Go ask the Bishop of Mexico to do this, tell him I have sent you," she says to him.

Juan Diego then travels to the city, to the palace of the Bishop where he begs an audience. He waits all day for the Bishop to speak with him and when he finally sees him, Juan Diego is put off, told to come back another time and tell his story again. And so he returns at day's end to the hill where "She" is waiting for him. Juan Diego tells her of his failure to make the Bishop understand and to get the building started.

"I beg of you, my Lady, my Queen, my Little Girl, (here begins the numerous and various names by which Our Lady is known), I beg of you, send one of your nobles to the palace."

"Do not doubt that I have many who will do my bidding but it must be you, Juan Diego. Go again tomorrow," she says.

Juan Diego goes back to the Bishop the next day. When the Bishop finally sees him, he asks for proof. He wants a sign to show that the Queen of Heaven has sent Juan Diego personally. Juan Diego says he will do this and leaves. This time the Bishop sends some of his staff to follow this pestering peasant, but a mist comes up and the followers lose sight of him on the hill. When they return to the Bishop, they are frustrated and angry and "fill the head of the Bishop with disbelief." They decide that if the peasant comes back again they will seize him and punish him for telling lies.

On his return to the hill, Juan Diego tells the Virgin of the Bishop's request for proof. She asks him to come back the next morning when she will supply him with proof to take to the Palace in the city.

When Juan Diego gets up the next day, he finds his uncle, with whom he lives and for whom he cares, to be very ill. The uncle asks him to go for a priest as he is sure he is going to die. Juan Diego hurries off. He thinks about taking another route to find the priest, a path which will bypass the place where he has seen the Virgin. When he is on the other side of the hill, he again encounters the Virgin coming down from the slope where first he saw her. "Where are you going, my son?" she asks. As soon as she hears his explanation she tells him not to worry, that his uncle is, in this minute, cured of all ills. (And so it was.)

The Lady tells him to go to the top of the hill and gather the flowers waiting for him there. He is to take these to the Bishop as proof and to ask once again, that a place of worship to the Queen of Heaven, be built on Tepeyac hill. Climbing to the top of the hill, Juan Diego wonders how there could be any flowers in this arid area, at this winter time of year. As soon as he thinks this, he becomes aware of a fragrance, the scent of flowers with the unmistakable blessing of the rose dominating. He hurries up and when he arrives at the place where he has seen the Virgin previously, there are roses, roses of Castile, alive, and beautiful, fragrant and bountiful. He gathers them up along with other flowers... dozens of blooms, and holding them in his cloak, his *tilma*. He hurries to the city. The fragrance intoxicates him as he returns for a third time to the palace of the Bishop.

This time when he arrives at the Palace he has his proof. Legend has it that the assistants to the Bishop can smell the fragrance of the blooms Juan Diego gently carries in his cloak and they are curious. "What have you got there?" they want to know. Juan

THE QUEEN OF MEXICO

Diego says he will only show what he has to the Bishop. He is quickly shown into the audience room, and when he opens his *tilma*, out pours the glorious blossoms, and there on his humble cloak, a cloak made out of rough cactus fibers, is the very image of the Queen of Heaven, the same as he has seen up close and personal on the hill of Tepeyac. Those assembled are agog over the flowers; then they see and marvel at the image on the cloth. Within a few months a sacred place is built for the Queen of Heaven, the Virgin of Guadalupe on the Tepeyac Hill.

The beleaguered Indians take to this new image of faith and hope with alacrity. There were many aspects to the Virgin and her symbolism which immediately spoke to the indigenous people in their pain and bewilderment, and they still do to this day. The Virgin of Guadalupe listens to you with compassion and asks nothing in return. She is a comfort when all about you is falling apart. Not least among the joys she showed to the people by the image on the *tilma*, was the clear recognition of a new person, a person of mixed blood ... the first mestiza.

∽

This is just the first part of the story, of how She showed herself to Juan Diego, how the basilica to her glory came to be built. There are many more stories, stories of how the image on the *tilma* of a humble Mexica has come to be recognized around the world and reproduced in millions of iterations by thousands of artists and devotees both humble and famous. There are many other stories concerning the miracle of the image on the *tilma*. The image has endured; it has been explained in many different ways. After 473 years and counting, the colors of the image are still fresh, the cloth of rough cactus fiber is still whole. How can that be when in attempts to replicate the *tilma*, nothing has come even close to matching its endurance? The image has been investigated, studied and subjected to experiments by various scientists and mystics and church officials and yet it remains a mystery. The image of Our Lady has led armies, inspired a nation and comforted the weary. It now hangs in a new basilica, under glass, visited every year by millions of faithful and hopeful worshipers from around the world. The attraction of the Virgin of Guadalupe is universal and complete ... she is truly the Queen of Heaven, the Queen of Mexico.

Post Script:
A note about Tepeyac Hill where the vision appeared to Juan Diego; where the basilica to the Virgin was built and subsequently rebuilt; where before the Euro hordes arrived, the mother of the Mexica gods, Tonantzin, was very actively worshiped. In other words, Tepeyac Hill is a place to which for thousands of years, billions of people have made their way as pilgrims in order to honor the sacred feminine. Thousands of years and billions of visitors have left an aura on the hill, palpably felt by the many who have visited there.

P.P.S.: Juan Diego died in 1548 at the age of 74, 17 years after the Queen of Heaven first appeared to him. He was canonized in 2002 as the first indigenous saint in the Roman Catholic Church.

Thanks to:
Carla Zarebska – *Guadalupe*
Eryk Hanut – *The Road to Guadalupe*
Francis Johnston – *The Wonder of Guadalupe*
The Internet – *various*

MARYETTA ACKENBOM

The Cross in the Tree

A few years ago, when I was still able to walk a couple of miles for exercise, I stopped short on the dirt jogging track at the Salvador Alvarado Stadium in Merida when a couple of young boys ran up to me. I shied away from them at first, thinking they meant mayhem, but one cried out to me in Spanish, "Wait! Wait *seño*! There's a cross..."

My Spanish was not perfect but I certainly understood that. I knew that "*seño*" was a respectful generic form used to address a woman of any age. So, I answered, "What cross? Where is the cross?"

"Right over there, on the tree. Come and see!"

"Wait, who are you?"

"I'm Juan, he's my cousin Pedro."

I was reluctant to interrupt my walking, but curious. I followed the two boys—both about ten years old and dressed in shorts and reasonably clean tee-shirts. I was no longer fearful.

They led me to a large *flamboyan*, called Royal Poinciana in

English. There, on a limb which I could reach if I stretched, there was fastened a cross, made from two heavy twigs tied together with stout sisal twine. The twine extended around the branch, holding the cross at an upright position. Plain, simple, disturbing.

"Why is it here?" I asked the boys.

"My dad told me it was here. We came to look for it." Juan rubbed his eyes, leaving traces of boy-grime around them.

"What did your dad say about it?"

"He said it was to remember a guy who died."

"What guy?"

"Dad didn't know. He just said to go look at it and remember it."

Pedro was dancing up and down, eager to tell me. "I think the guy killed himself. I heard something about that."

A young man dressed for jogging joined us. "It's quite a legend," he said. "The cross has been here for a few years."

I turned toward the man as the boys skipped away. "What is the story, sir?"

"A young student named Ramon was an excellent runner. He trained long and hard for a special race that was being held here. The winner would go to Mexico City to compete in a national event."

I gasped. "Don't tell me…"

"He woke up the morning of the race feeling sick, but he raced anyway, and lost. During that evening, before the park was closed for the night, he hanged himself from that tree."

Wide-eyed, I asked, "Who put the cross there?"

"His father. He blamed himself for the boy's death. He felt he had pushed him too hard to excel. A few years later, the father also committed suicide. The cross commemorates them both."

I looked at the man's face, and then looked down. "A double tragedy. Did you know the family?"

"I am Ramon's younger brother. I helped my father fasten the cross to the tree." He turned to leave.

I thanked the man and slowly walked home through the shady streets, deep in thought.

THERESA DIAZ GRAY

A Very Mérida Christmas

Jasmine perfume filtered into the house, announcing Katti's presence as clearly as her voice and precise diction. After the usual round of *buenos dias*, air kisses, inquiries regarding everyone's health, and the hundreds of other polite things you say here before you ever get to the real reason for the visit, Katti firmly announced, "Of course you are coming to Christmas dinner at my parents' house."

Katti had been the first person we met in Merida, knocking on our door our first morning, introducing herself and her four-year-old daughter, Katita. Standing four feet nine inches tall if you include the enormous mane of curls piled on her head and maybe weighing ninety pounds, she's such a self-assured person, it's always a shock to realize how tiny she is. When we met her, she was temporarily living for free in her brother's house while he paid to live elsewhere. Her sister, Isis Amor, who everyone called Amor, operated a restaurant on their front porch every day except Sunday. Daily, Katti made her rounds, calling on every business within a half hour's walk. She would march up to the counter, name the day's dishes and ask which one they wanted to eat today. She would then walk back, pack the lunches and deliver them. From noon onwards she waited tables until the food ran out, usually around two. Between Amor's cooking and Katti's unique sales style, they did very well for the three years Katti lived there. She also cut hair and did makeup on the side.

Fortunately for us, she had taken us under her wing. As the oldest of five children, she was used to being in charge and though she is at least ten years younger than me, she would advise me about where to shop, which was the best ham (*pierna marca Kir*), the best cheese (*manchego, marca Gonela*), and where to buy fresh milk. She had adopted us as part of her extended family. I have no idea what the rest of the family thought about it, but in her book that meant we were coming for Christmas dinner, no ifs, ands, or buts about it.

I tried to explain that we didn't keep Christmas, but got bogged down. Katti already knew that I had been raised Catholic and my husband, Protestant, so she couldn't fathom why we didn't celebrate the holiday. Like babes in the woods, we were too new to Merida and Mexico to know that we should have just accepted the invitation, no matter what our real intentions were.

As the designated Spanish speaker, it fell upon me to do most of the talking, so I dutifully asked, "What time should we come over on Christmas?" Once again, I understood all the individual words but had no idea what we were talking about. After a lot of back and forth, I finally understood that Christmas dinner was at midnight on Christmas Eve not on Christmas day.

"Midnight is very late for us, I don't know if we will still be awake then," I tried to ease our way out of attending.

"No problem, we will bring the party to your house. I doubt that you will be able to sleep with all the music, you should come and enjoy the party rather than just hear it through the walls." Katti smiled showing her strong white teeth, knowing that she had won that round, as she watched my husband's mouth drop open. Appalled at the idea of being able to hear a party through two foot thick walls I accepted defeat and promised that we would attend. I couldn't narrow down the time frame to anything clearer than "come about an hour before dinner."

My holiday mood improved greatly when I spotted bottles of *sidra real* (royal cider) at the grocery store, I bought some to take to the party. As a first generation Cuban-American, I grew up drinking Martinelli's sparkling apple cider at the holidays, but this was hard cider imported from Spain, more like champagne than apple juice. Even more exciting was the discovery of, not one, but all three types of Spanish almond nougat, *turrón,* none of which made it to the party. When I was a child, my mother made an annual pilgrimage to San Francisco at Christmas time to shop at Casa Lucas in the Mission district, bringing back *turrón,* along with other seasonal delicacies imported from Spain. My son, like me, prefers the a*licante* type but since Husband had never tasted any of the confections, I thought it was only fair to give him the opportunity to choose his own favorite. The combination of honey and almonds, no matter how it's done, is addicting, whether it's the brittle white *alicante,* the soft fudge-like brown *jijona,* or the yellowish stiffer *yema. Turrón* is my kryptonite.

Green as grass, we arrived promptly at eleven. None of the other guests were there yet. The five of us sat awkwardly on the pretty but uncomfortable living room set crammed into the small *sala* between a gigantic nativity scene dominating one corner and an enormous Christmas tree occupying the opposite one. Husband had on his fanciest white embroidered *guayabera*, I was decked out in my only dress and a pair of high heels, and *Mijo* (*Mi hijo*, my son, is affectionately contracted into Mijo in Spanish) was dressed in his customary black from head to toe. We all felt uncomfortably out of place, but at least we were dressed appropriately. Katti was poured into a slinky black dress and Katita looked like the top of a wedding cake, totally adorable in a Christmas plaid, complete with a big bow in her sleek brown pageboy. Since I was the only one who spoke any Spanish at that time, the burden of trying to make small talk with Katti and Katita fell on my shoulders. We all smiled politely while trying to think of something to say, while the three Isises worked in the kitchen, Isis Azalea, Katti's mother, who we respectfully called Doña Isis, Katti's sister, Isis Amor, who as I mentioned before, went by Amor, and Katti's daughter, Isis Socorro, who logically should have been called Socco but went by Isis. As teenagers do, Mijo quickly left us to our own devices when one of his English speaking friends arrived.

Fortunately for us, small children are more than willing to charm strange adults with their talents and knowledge. A miniature version of her mother, Katita started to point out all the different parts of the crèche and give us the history of some of the more esoteric pieces. I gravely inspected the scene. Noticing that the manger was empty, I asked where the baby Jesus was.

"He isn't born yet, so he won't be there until midnight," she giggled, bringing up her hands to hide her pixie-like face in embarrassment. Her huge black eyes opening wide to emphasize her seriousness, Katita explained the tradition of everyone taking turns rocking the baby Jesus figurine in their arms while singing a special song, illustrating the motions for us. She was very excited because this year she was going to have the great honor of placing the baby in the manger.

She confided that now that she had attained the advanced age of five, she also was going to spend a week at her father's house starting on Christmas day. Convinced that she had my husband firmly wrapped around her little finger, she took his hands in hers, telling him in a serious voice, "But do not despair, I promise that I will return in a week." With that sentence she succeeded in winning his heart. Katita has a fine Latin sense of the dramatic and tremendous charm.

While all this was going on, people kept arriving. We had thought that this was going to be a small family dinner. Both of us grew up in large families; we should have known better. We met cousins, uncles and aunts. We met neighbors who had lived side by side for so many generations they may as well have been family. Then there were the neighborhood kids who had married and moved away, they had to stop in and pay respects while on their way to their own family functions. Katti's oldest brother, his wife and three kids arrived late, having eaten dinner with his mother-in-law. Out of politeness, they ate another dinner.

Swept along by the incoming tide of people, the party had by that time relocated outside to the totally unrecognizable backyard. Gone were the laundry lines propped up on forked sticks and hung with everyone in the extended family's clothing. In its place were strings of white Christmas lights and banners made of paper squares cut like Christmas snowflakes but in more intricate designs called *papel picado*. I've since learned that you can buy papel picado bunting for all sorts of occasions from birthday parties to Day of the Dead, but this was my introduction to it and I was fascinated. Under the lights were two long rows of plastic tables which had been pushed together to form one elongated table. They must have been relocated from the *cocina economica* that Amor ran during the week. Two were borrowed from the store next door that Don Ernesto (Katti's father) owned. The rest obtained from who knows where else with their matching plastic chairs because there was seating for at least thirty people, all in festive Coca Cola red, covered with long white plastic table cloths.

If it wasn't for the fact that people came and went, there still wouldn't have been enough chairs. Neighbors and family stopped by on their way to other parties. Food kept appearing out of the kitchen, including a huge brown and succulent turkey, that later I learned, had to be sent out for roasting at one of the local bakeries because Doña Isis's oven wasn't big enough. There was spaghetti, covered in a bland tomato sauce and cooked into submission. Tasty *ensalada rusa*, (Russian salad) a potato salad with peas, carrots, celery, and other things not found in potato salads north of the border combined with McCormick mayonnaise, that contains lemon juice and tastes to me like Miracle Whip salad dressing. There were potato chips, black bean dip, salsa, and guacamole. There was cake, I'm sure of it but I don't remember it. That party was where I tasted my first and unfortunately not my last *sandwichon*. I can understand why Cuban-American cuisine might be stuck in the pre-Castro fifties, but no one has ever explained to my satisfaction how the *sandwichon*, like the duck-billed platypus, has managed to outlive its era. *Sandwichon* is a variation of the 1940's ribbon sandwich, loaves of white bread, crusts removed then sliced horizontally, each layer spread with ham pate and other interesting things then frosted with dressing or cream cheese. I have even sampled one that contained a layer that appeared to have been concocted from condensed split pea soup. Some of them alternate strawberry jam with the meat pate, which can be made of any sort of meat, but deviled ham seems to predominate. *Sandwichon* is memorable.

Just after midnight, a tremendous pounding rattled the front door, which had mysteriously closed after being wide open all evening. All the cousins and other assorted neighborhood children raced to be the first to open it. In front of the door, leaning against the stoop there slumped an enormous red satin sack full of presents, freshly delivered by Santa Claus! Each child had a present with their name on it. While the kids happily opened their gift, one of the parents quietly explained that a neighbor played Santa. The neighborhood parents would drop off the wrapped presents in the morning, then dressed in a red Santa Suit with all the trimmings the neighbor would then deliver presents. Jorge, our neighborhood *Papá Noel* also worked in the big Winter Wonderland that Coca Cola sponsored every year in the Carrefour (now Chedraui Selecto) parking lot across the street from Gran Plaza Mall.

Eventually, someone started to play music and the dancing began. Katti's ex-husband asked her to dance, it was amazing. He is very handsome in a dark Latin way; it was obvious that there was still a lot of feeling there. The sparks were flying and infecting the other dancers. An impromptu salsa contest started.

I don't know how, but somehow, the party spilled out of the house and into the street. Young people sat on the steps, flirting and drinking Coca Cola, while a lone open topped police truck cruised slowly down the street, the four officers in the back looked up as they arrived at the stop sign on the corner. They all were slumped in their seats, obviously tired but still managing to grin as they watched one of the girls trying to teach her brother how to dance.

At three in the morning, Husband and I went home, leaving our teenage son at the party. He came home shortly after us, but the party went on. Before we fell asleep in our hard rental bed, Husband turned to me and said, "I think this was my best Christmas ever."

The next day, our street was quiet, no traffic, just some wrapping paper rolling down the deserted road...

Things have changed in our neighborhood. Doña Isis has passed on. Two years ago, Katti's brother married and moved into his own house, he had to renovate and make the house unlivable first, but that is another story for another day. Amor no longer runs a restaurant on her brother's front porch, she's also married and moved to a more fashionable neighborhood in the north. Katti relocated around the corner; her older children no longer live with her, little Katita is a teenager and more interested in charming the boys than her gringo neighbors. Mijo speaks fluent Spanish now, but is living in California. We no longer rent next door to Don Ernesto's store and home. Now we own a house across the street, next to Katti's brother.

There isn't a big party in Don Ernesto's house on Christmas Eve anymore; it's found a new location with another branch of the family, in another part of town. Instead, my husband and I have an annual open house on Christmas day, it's fun but much more subdued. If you're in the neighborhood, you should stop by. There might not be salsa dancing until dawn but there will be salsa.

CHERIE PITTILLO

My Line Full of Memories

Our day started like most Wednesdays in our casa; the housekeeper and her daughter, Abi and Abi Dos, arrived at 9 AM, more or less, full of smiles that reached their eyes; they shared their lightness of spirit, and yet performed as professionals in their work.

About two hours later my husband called me to look at termites that Abi found in our home. I peered behind our sideboard in our dining room and saw the telltale trail of the dark brown, miniature-like mole hill that contained those tiny terrorists. That path encompassed and protected the damn critters from light as they marched to their war zone of destruction. It seemed to ooze out of our wall at its joint with the floor. That foot long trail met the foot of our sideboard to lead up into my sacred storage of some sentimental possessions.

Slowly, we began to assess the damage as we pulled out from the sideboard henequen placemats from the Yucatan, colorful hand-loomed placemats from San Cristobal de las Casas, and then I saw the attack on my mother lode of memories. Somehow these creatures of the dark missed my Granny's twelve inch wooden bowl and her wooden butter press, but the hungry horde etched crevasses into her eight inch long wooden paddle. Granny had used that paddle to pound any watery milk out of the butter in that bowl. She then pressed the butter into a half pound trapezoid shape, put the butter mold over it, and pushed down the plunger. That action left an impression of a sheaf of wheat on top of the butter mound.

I almost cried when I saw egg masses attached to a delicate white porcelain pitcher with Wedgewood blue flowers dotted on it along with its matching platter. Those two items go back five generations, and I've kept them for inspiration whether I lived in Africa, the US or Mexico. My great, great grandmother sheared a sheep, carded the wool, and wove a yard of fabric to barter it for those two pieces of china. To me they symbolize the ingenuity and determination to work for something that your heart yearns for.

Other pieces such as a platter from my Grandma and my Mama's cake plate and serving knife were untouched.

However, the destruction continued. Adjacent to my porcelain memories were tatted, crocheted, and embroidered linens by my Granny and my Aunt.

My husband then attacked the sideboard with anti-termite spray in what I would call determined vengeance.

Meanwhile, I think the caring housekeeper saw my saddened face and gently offered to wash this mountain of remembrances in the form of handkerchiefs, table runners, tablecloths, and napkins. She and her daughter cleaned up the china first as I shared with them my stories about the wooden items and the dishes. As they tackled the linens, I hung them up on our clothesline under our covered terrace. I pondered

MY LINE FULL OF MEMORIES

about the hands that created versus my hands on the computer as I typed. I wondered how my Granny taught my aunt to embroider. How old was she when she learned? Did her mother teach her or an older sister? How old was my aunt? Mama taught me several types of embroidery stitches when I was in the fifth grade. I remember I was a reluctant student to be indoors learning these intricate thread patterns when the world of nature always beckoned me outside our front door.

I also thought of the contrast of the cross-stitching I see in the Yucatan and now how the sewing machine embroiders the *huipils* (traditional Maya dress) much faster. I wonder if we lose some of the love when we lose the touch of direct contact between our hands and fabric.

A slight breeze blew softly on the terrace and lifted up colors of these varied cloths on my clothesline like a rainbow arc. My soul uplifted too and I gave thanks for those who created this line full of memories.

GWEN LANE

Time Divine or Define Time

In English we call it a birthday, yet, we mile-stone our journey upon this planet in years not days, although, it is acceptable to add the amount of months to your age when very young or very old. In Spanish we say *Cumple anos* or completion of years. Would we have a different perspective about our time if we considered our passage in days? Next time someone asks me how old I am, I will say, "My body and spirit have been united together over 18,000 days." I hope a kind soul replies, "You don't look a day over 15,000."

Perhaps we could define time as duration of events or things that pass from a state of potentially in the future, through the present, to finality in the past.

I paced my roof top garden as I often do on warm, star-filled nights when I can't sleep and thought how the pace of life differs in Yucatan from other places. Schools, businesses, religions run on appointed time but social time rules relax. If a friend asked you over for a fiesta at 8:00 pm and you arrive at

8:30, it that too early or fashionable late? The Canadians are known to arrive ten minutes early, those from the United Stated arrive on time but Yucatecos arrive around one hour late. When those from north of the border get together, events sometimes need clarification, appointed time or Yucatan time.

Is time a fabrication of existence or only the rotation of the Earth? Could one connect with the pulse of Earth by listening for the vibrations through time? Perhaps, the Yucatecos spirits are time tuned into these various vibrations.

How do you measure time? Time of day, time frame, timeline, time warp, time passage, daytime, nighttime, dream time; is there a map of time to consult if one gets lost in time? Can you buy or lose or find time, if time is of the essence?

After living in Yucatan a few months, we accepted an invitation to a family fiesta on the other side of town. We circled around trees and parks looking for the elusive home of our friends. We wandered around side streets that sent us many blocks out of our way and often ended. We asked for guidance and every helpful clue we received from the locals led us in a different direction. We got lost in time without a map.

Somebody had to be the first guests and forty minutes after the appointed time, we found our destination. After our host greeted us with warm hugs and kisses he explained an easier way to find their home.

When I heard our hostess had just stepped into the shower, my face turned pinker than a Yucatan sunset. Except for the bickering between the driver and the navigator, roaming around a little longer, getting to know some new streets sounded like a good idea right then. They said 8 not 9. If they meant, don't arrive till 9, why didn't they say it?

At 11:30 our stomachs moaned for a heavier food than chips, dips and veggies. The host returned from a local restaurant with platters of grilled chicken, succulent *arrachera* beef, *al pastor* and other meats, bowls of mild and spicy green and red sauces, guacamole, limes, stacks of tortillas, onion, peppers, tomatoes, tamales. The feast began.

By the time the main course or *plato fuerte*, strong plate as we call it here, arrived, the sight of a small child tucked away on a blanket and pillows in a corner of the dining or living room reminded me of how differently a child measures time. All of time is the moment, the present. Older children played hide and seek, tag, basketball and other games and activities.

As we left at one in the morning with sleepy children, our host introduced us to people who just arrived. Sometimes fiestas can turn into a two day event or definitely into the early morning hours.

As I waited at home all day for the promised cable repair person who never showed up, I wondered if time is all in the mind. Time is absolute in the sense that time of an event is independent of the observer or the observers' frame of reference. Why do some hours seem longer or shorter than others? Can time stand still? Or, is time all a perspective?

∞

I met the family that invited us to the fiesta at a kindergarten parent meeting when we bonded together with two other families as the carrot group. Fortunately for me, one other carrot moms knew some English and with my limited Spanish I could almost keep up with the plans and ideas.

During the school year each parent/vegetable group had two opportunities to assist the teacher and prepare a one hour lesson and games for the whole class. It took us a lot of time and many meetings to prepare a one hour experience. Our planning meetings took place at a family friendly restaurant, meaning a place centrally located, that had play equipment for the children and didn't mind if you monopolized a few tables for hours. The meetings went something like this:

First hour, waited for everyone to show up. Second hour, ordered food, ate and talked about anything except plans for our project. Third and sometimes fourth hour, leisurely over dessert and coffee, ideas got discussed and assignments made.

We sang a short song about how much time to spend daily brushing their teeth and washing their hands and taught it to them. Our lesson revolved around good dental and hand hygiene and we used our time to play a matching memory game with big cards in the shapes of hands and teeth. Each child took home a handmade matching number game card set, zero to nine, in the shape of teeth. My job consisted of copying and cutting out all the teeth, writing one number and its spelling in English and Spanish on each tooth and packaging them for twenty-five children.

Mayas used the shapes and stars and planets in the sky as a method of measuring and tracked time by the heavens. They considered the capture of the history and the mystery of time and its involvement in all things continuous, the utmost importance to their knowledge that space and time intertwine. Mayas viewed time in cycles; they based their calendar on advanced astronomical observations.

Eventually I learned to relax time and melt into Yucatan time. When we accepted an invitation to an 8 pm wedding at a hacienda 20 minutes outside of town, we knew, by that time, it meant arrive at 8:30 for good seats. The plato fuerte arrived around midnight, we chose not to stay till breakfast at four in the morning. No matter how early or late you arrive to a party or event, the plato fuerte will not be served until around midnight.

If you're used to eating early, best to plan on having a snack before you go.

What controls the movements of the heavens of time? Is it an unseen creativity and endless energy that will remain long after time has turned our blood and bone into dust and mineral? Whatever it is, I'm sure the fire within the human spirit will always rise up and triumph.

Time is a peculiar thing. If our host rock travels through time and space, doesn't that make us space and time travelers? Do we pass through time or does time pass through us?

Time cannot be money because time is eternal. Yucatecos take time to remember that everyday our dance of life swings precariously. They take the time to clear mind clutter, recharge and renew, to put heart and soul back into life. They know our divine time on earth together one day ends. Every day is the present, a gift to be cherished and savored.

LORRAINE BAILLIE BOWIE

A Woman of a Certain Age

A soul burns bright in the Yucatan.

Crisp white linen, now stained with age, falls to the softness yearned for in her youth. The harsh pulling and pushing of life stretched and wrinkled her fabric to the ultimate rendering of both exposed and receptive. Exposed are the colors kept safe behind the shield, slowly burning for release.

Bushy bright colors of a tail relentless in its wagging peek through the loosened threads, no longer worried about a judgment. Brilliant amber and gold fused with the radiance of white light steadily churns toward the open windows in the weave. Amber, swirling beyond the safety of old linen, finds fuchsia giggling and brown guffawing to a story told by the intellectual dark green. The longing blue of lost love lingers with the contented lilac. The purple of passion soars with a scream of magenta while the lavender of passion-remembered whispers to the impudent scarlet.

UNIQUELY YUCATAN

The colors of amber linger at the edge. Will the brilliance of the array extinguish her emerging flame or will she be enhanced by her joining? With the energy of her radiant amber, she leaps into the panorama of colors, willing to extinguish or perhaps to burn brighter.

LORNA GAIL DALLIN

Blanche and the Big Cry

The taxi headlights sweep down the driveway to her coach house, glinting off the beveled panes of glass in the front door. Home!

She exits the taxi, makes one last check of the interior to see if anything has been left, then counts the number of pieces of luggage the taxi driver has just deposited on the porch. The driver offers to carry the bags inside for her, she declines the offer, pays the fare and adds a generous tip.

"I can handle this," says Blanche. She has a special way she likes to unlock the door and enter into her house when she returns after her travels. She loves the feeling of expectancy as she steps inside her home. All so familiar, she flips her arm off to the right and her hand goes directly to the light switch and turns on. She looks around her and is drawn to her image in the mirror beside the front hall closet. She steps over to the mirror and has a good look. There she is, Blanche Forsythe, looking tan and fit. A smile breaks out when she contemplates the summery, tropical clothes she wears, soon to be packed away and replaced with big city darks and pastels. She looks pretty good, she thinks. Without a doubt the 6 weeks she has just spent in Mexico have put a glow upon her. "The last bloom," she thinks, and turns away from her image.

In the kitchen, Blanche makes herself a pot of tea and checks in the cupboard for biscuits. Yes, all there, some of her favorites even. Hope there aren't any weevils in the cookies. Again, she chuckles; eating a bug or two couldn't be any stranger than some of the things she ingested over the past weeks at the Mexican clinic. She had done it all, everything expected and advised for her regime of cancer management. "If there are bugs in the biscuits, so be it!"

She pours the perfectly brewed tea into her favorite cup, takes a moment to snuffle in the aroma of Earl Grey, then moves to the kitchen window seat. She flips on another light which bathes the garden at the side of the house in a soft glow from which emerges a bed of swaying daffodils; the tulips are already past bloom and drooping. "Do I have the instincts of a tulip?" she wonders. Again she thinks of the last bloom and her spirits sag. She stands, holding the still warm cup of tea against her chest, then moves to the kitchen chaise and sinks down into the familiar comfort of her grandmother's favorite chair. There is a little whimper waiting to build into a cry, lurking about her. Will she indulge? She might run it into a real rip-snorter. But no, she had her last really big cry many years ago. The story of that cry always enlivens her for some reason. Perhaps it is because she remembers it so well even though it happened over 20 years ago. It always makes her smile when she recalls it.

It's a good story, an uplifting story, even if it is about crying. In the late 1980's, she had been living in a palapa on Isla Mujeres, "Jewel of the Mexican Caribbean," on the east side of the island, right on the edge, looking out to sea. She liked to describe her lifestyle at that time as "voluntary simplicity". When people asked what she did there, what was she doing, she would tell them "my life is my work of art", and often she believed it herself. One casual visitor to her palapa by the sea was overheard to say when leaving, "She lives like an Okie!" She had to ask someone to explain Okie to her.

This simple life (no electricity and all that implies) had attracted two dogs to her home, somewhat isolated as it was. Her "company", she called the dogs. There was Mama Dog-o, a prime example of the Dobermaya breed of the Yucatan, and there was Daddy Dog-o, a large, substantial, black lab-something mix. She knew them as a team. The dogs came and went as they pleased and were often at her palapa during the heat of the day taking advantage of the cool shade of the porch and the fresh breeze off the Caribbean Sea. She had heard from several people on the island that Daddy had once been taken to the mainland and "left" by his owners who no longer wanted such a large dog. He found his way back onto the island and was considered a free agent now. Blanche had watched one afternoon at a beach restaurant as Daddy Dog-o came in off the beach and headed straight to the table of a tourist couple eating there. Daddy sat by the table and gave an authoritative, rumble-y WOOF! And the young blonde woman immediately dropped half her fish fillet onto the sand floor for him. Daddy did not hesitate and wolfed it down.

Blanche had been living on the island for about three and a half years repairing a broken heart, a disrupted life; by reading, puttering, and doing a bit of travelling in the Yucatan. Life repairs were going not too badly. She recalled that at the time of this story she had been having a good deal of fun with some visiting sailors. She had done a bit of sailing herself so enjoyed the yacht-y set; they were (almost) all good storytellers. The Florida to Isla Mujeres Regatta was just winding down and one of the visitors had taken a shine to her. What fun – what a balm to her still slightly bruised and fragile sense of self. She thought she remembered the "sailor's" name as George. He told great stories and liked to neck. Oh Boy! So did she. "A Regatta Romance", everyone sails away at the end of the meet. Right? She was well aware that this was just some fun, a fling ... really, no problems. Anyway, she was looking forward to her friend Renee, coming down to the island in one week. Blanche had a Birthday coming up and she meant to celebrate well with her friend.

So when the regatta was over and she had taken "George" to the ferry so's he could return to his Florida life, she was surprised and unprepared when a deluge of tears broke over her on her return to her palapa home. It started with a little bit of feeling sorry for herself, and soon blossomed into a "poor me" ... all by herself again. A wailing session was soon underway. She couldn't have stopped it if she tried and she didn't. She just let it all out.

At some point in this tempest of tears, she found herself sitting on the small cliff at the bottom of her property, looking out to sea, a watery view into which she hurled her sobs and blubberings and moans along with her snot and tears. Soon she was yelling and the yells turned to howls.

Suddenly, she became aware of something beside her, a presence to her left. Was someone actually there? Out of the corner of her eye, she could see ... oh my gawd; it was Daddy Dog-O! There he was, sitting up close to her, leaning slightly on her shoulder. He was looking out to sea. As she turned to him, he turned to look at her; their eyes met, then he leaned over and licked her on the side of her face. She stopped crying and put her arm across his back. They sat there for a few moments more, both looking at the view of billowy cloud and azure sea as she subsided from the sobs, then drooped. Daddy Dog-O heaved a little sigh, stood up and ambled off. She was spent. She would have to sit for a minute before getting up. She lay back on a bed of rock and sand – what an outstanding metaphor, she thought, for her life to date. Blanche let the Caribbean breeze dry the snot on her face and when it was time, she got up, went in to her palapa by the sea and made some lunch.

And that was it, the last big cry. She guessed that she just cried it all out that day, no more tears left for this life. And there weren't. Oh, perhaps a little tightness at the back of the throat during a tear-jerker movie, or a slight prickling of the eyes in a sentimental moment ... but no more blubbering and howling, thank gawd. A few months later she returned to Canada, her rustic life on a Jewel of a Caribbean Island set aside but fondly remembered. And from that time by the sea, Blanche still felt the blessings bestowed on her by Mexico; enough sun and light, enough warm sand, and enough irritants to balance so well with enough joys and revelations. And perhaps best of all, there had been a dog to lick her face to let her know that she was not alone in this world.

"Enough of this maundering," she says, and stands up from the chaise, the tea now cold in her cup. Her hand goes to her cheek where the dog licked her. "I can handle this," she murmurs. Then Blanche straightens and says out loud in her most forceful Upper Canada/University of Toronto Cheerleader voice, "I can handle this!" and goes to find a warmer cup of tea.

CHERIE PITTILLO

Wren Ovation

The Yucatan Wren
Yucatan Wren, *Campylorhynchus yucatanicus,* Matraca yucateca
(Spanish)

Why should the Yucatan Wren receive a standing ovation? As an endemic species, it doesn't exist anywhere else on earth! This unique, native bird lives along a narrow strip of the northern coast of the Yucatan state from the Celestun Biosphere Reserve* to El Cuyo. On one hand, that's an exciting claim. On the other, coastal development threatens its limited range. That would be heart-wren-ching.

This striped, streaked, spotted, seven-inch species is a master of camouflage in its coastal, dry scrub habitat. The first time I saw it, I called it a Cactus Wren as cacti were near its low perch. Scientists previously identified it as a subspecies of the Cactus Wren, but now confirm it as a separate species.

The Yucatan Wren forages in pairs or small groups on the ground and in low vegetation. References don't agree whether it only eats insects, but also lizards and fruits.

I've photographed these wrens off sandy roads in Celestun, across from the old shrimp farm in Sisal, and in the cactusey, thorny scrub from Chuburna Puerto to Telchac Puerto. I'm especially fond of a couple that lives on the grounds of a secluded beach hotel near Telchac. Usually their wren-dition of several calls greet me and then I search the undergrowth to locate them. The first time I heard their raspy, husky growls, I thought of monkeys chattering or two people fussing at each other.

One study found that the male Yucatan Wren builds several nests and wrenders one to a female for their wrendezvous. Although he is a master of wrenovation, he doesn't wrent the other nests.

Another study indicates the male constructs nests about four to six feet above ground in eleven species of trees from the coastal dunes to the mangrove forest. Of those trees, 75% of the nests occur in only three tree species. That dependency also limits their range.

Just like the Yucatan Wren, go wrenew your outdoor appreciation with a friend or friends. Go coastal!

*The Celestun Biosphere Reserve also includes part of the extreme NW Campeche state.

DISCLAIMER: *References do not agree on details about this species. Here are my resources: A Guide to the Birds of Mexico and Northern Central America, Birds and Reserves of the Yucatan Peninsula, Common Birds of the Yucatan Peninsula,* http://macaulaylibrary.org/, *a website from Cornell Lab of Ornithology,* http://www.bioone.org/doi/abs/10.1676/08-164.1?journalCode=wils, http://ibc.lynxeds.com/species/yucatan-wren-campyl orhynchus- yucatanicus, http://neotropical.birds.cornell.edu/portal/species/ overview?p_p_spp=529836

First published in The Yucatan Times, Backyard Birding in Merida, Yucatan and Beyond

MARYETTA ACKENBOM

On the Beach

My friend Lucia has a house on the beach, in Progreso, a half-hour's drive from Merida.
Lucia loves being at the beach. Since childhood, she has spent two or three months every summer in one beach house or another, raising five children and hosting numerous grandchildren. She still says she lives in Progreso, although the original summertime community has gradually moved eastward along the coast, and her present house is a breezy three-bedroom in the town of Chicxulub. Leafy oleanders surround the house, and the yard is thickly planted with sea-grape trees. Iguanas and other lowlifes run through the ground cover.

The summer vacation at the beach is a tradition among citified people who live in Merida. Lucia also spends the two-week Easter vacation there, and a few days at Christmas. Her family's original house was on the western side of Progreso, along with two blocks of other row-houses inhabited by family members. Porches formed open corridors, allowing the families to visit freely. Children and their nannies ran as wild as they liked. Two or three piers led from the beach to where the water was just deep enough to accommodate a fishing boat.

Until 1947, a ferry provided the only transportation between Yucatan and the rest of Mexico, and even that ferry could not dock at the shallow piers of Progreso—or at any other seaside village. The ferry and other large boats would anchor about three miles out into the gulf, and passengers and goods would be carried to and fro by small boats. Lucia and other travelers would take the familiar ferry, the "Emancipacion," when they needed to visit the country's capital.

Lucia is aging (as are we all), and she has the additional problem of being almost completely blind. Years ago she could run her household on the beach by herself with a daily maid. Now, she must have someone with her all the time.

I have been invited to be that someone several times. The first time it was grand. We spent an hour or two in the water, covered with sunblock, and many hours relaxing in the house and on the patio—and eating. We also enjoyed watching the pelicans and gulls, soaring and diving for fish. The pleasure boats of vacationers contrasted with the local fishing boats and busy wave-runners. The gulf waters changed color by the hour, from yellow-green to olive, then blue-green. Farther out toward the horizon, the deep waters became purple and almost black. The setting sun was always special, sometimes glorious.

The second and third times she invited me, I was not that anxious to accompany Lucia. I preferred to stay in my Merida house, visiting Lucia a time or two for a day—one day—at the beach. I began to find it boring, even for a day.

Every day, Lucia and any visitors would wade out about a hundred yards through the shallow water to swim—or rather to float and chat—where the water was deep enough to be fun.

One day I was alone with Lucia in the calm green water when her daughter cruised by in a motor boat and invited us aboard. Anita wanted to take us out beyond the end of the shipping pier, five miles out. The first part of the pier was about a mile long, and in water deep enough for the "Emancipacion" and small freighters to dock. It was completed in 1947 and served well for a number of years. Three expansion projects extended the pier to about five miles, large and deep enough for cruise ships to dock.

How to get onto Anita's boat? Anita jumped in the water and helped push two aging, plump swimmers over the stern. I didn't think we'd make it, but Anita insisted.

We enjoyed a refreshing ride out, nearing the docks where cruise ships let off their colorful passengers. Cargo ships unloaded goods from all over the world and took on local products for export.

Skies darkened. Fast. We were committed to the trip out when we realized that a summer storm rushed toward us. We rounded the pier as the rain and wind descended. The gray-green water surrounding us turned black.

The boat stalled. The rain was so heavy we couldn't see each other in the boat. We just had to float, and hope nothing came too near us.

The huge gray concrete arches of the pier loomed out of the downpour. Anita struggled with the motor. It coughed but did not start. We were going to hit the pier!

I was scared. Anita was scared, she admitted it later. Lucia—of course she smiled through the whole episode. Never did she admit fear. Her lack of sight was not the reason for her sang-froid. She simply seemed to enjoy the adventure!

The storm winds tossed the waves, and the boat. I told my unhappy stomach to behave. We had enough trouble.

Closer and closer to the arches we bobbed, up and down with the waves. Anita grabbed a long pole I hadn't noticed, releasing it from its fastening along the side of the boat. We closed with the pier and Anita gave a strong push against the concrete with the pole, enough to make the boat veer away. Torrential rain continued to fall. Away from the concrete arch, visibility was again nil. We could easily hit the other side of the arch, obscured by the weather.

But—we were now under the arch. It wasn't raining there. The wind pushed rain through the opening, keeping us saturated, but we began to see around us.

After again trying the boat's inboard motor with no luck, Anita moved aft where a small outboard hung. One push—it started, delighted to be of service. We continued through the arch to the east side of the pier.

It took three times as long for us to return to Lucia's house with the power of the outboard. I was cold, weary, wet and miserable. Anita kept up a chatter with her mother, but it seemed that, according to Lucia, she did not handle the boat correctly. She wanted to go home.

Lucia was also cold, wet, and miserable, explaining her miserable attitude. And I think, finally, she was also afraid. She sensed our fear and divined our predicament, in spite of Anita's attempt to soothe her.

Putt-putting back, we outran the storm, but rain still fell.

Somehow, Lucia knew when we were within sight of her house and she began to insist that Anita stop so we could get out.

Finally we were close enough to climb out and wade and swim to shore. Anita took the boat home, farther east along the coast, and then returned by land to make sure we were all right.

Lucia and I had bathed and dressed, and were happily watching the most spectacular sunset of the season, above and through the arches of the far-away shipping pier.

I somehow managed to have other commitments when Lucia again invited me to her beach house.

GWEN LANE

The Encounter

You came to me softly in the night. In my dreamy state, I heard your whisper close to my ear; telling of all the places on my body you longed to enter.

You hovered close to feel my warmth and gently touching my neck, slowly moving down my shoulder and back. You danced between my legs to find just the right spot.

You drove me crazy with anticipation of our next tussle, hands flaying, feet jerking, until at last, surrender. Finally I could bear no more and wrapped my body tight within the sheet to escape your engorged attraction and ravenous appetite for me.

In the morning you had left, as quiet and mysterious as you arrived.

The bumps and scratches of our torrid and sleepless night will linger in my memory for days. Damn Mosquito.

LORRAINE BAILLIE BOWIE

Roswell to Merida: the alien imperative

Ankle deep party trash embarrassed the sacred grounds of Uxmal, the famous Maya archeological site located in the heart of the Yucatan jungle. December 21, 2012, promised the end of the world and then reneged, but not before attracting planet-wide diverse groups of rowdy believers and non-believers. The curious crowds moved in random patterns, striving to display their members' bizarre individuality, yet offer a unified presence to the extraterrestrials they expected. If the aliens admired insanity, they would have been impressed. Since it appeared to most that they did not arrive, some say perhaps they whizzed away to saner planets.

At one end of the grounds, a man stooped from worry, straightened to clang a mallet against a bronze plate. The echo carried to the other side of the compound where a new arrival to the planet felt welcomed by the sound. The believers and non-believers were too busy simultaneously observing and participating in the parade to notice that the earth had gained one more adult resident.

Chars4 hid his onion skin nakedness behind a tool shed on the fringe of the main grounds. Seeing no one in his vicinity, he folded over his 6'7" frame in order to access the subcutaneous communication device implanted under the skin of his left ankle.

Pressing the gadget with his forefinger, he said, "Sola, you dropped me here naked and as tall as two indigenous people stacked on top of each other like a totem pole. Did you miss the class on human characteristics? I'm a senior operative, what did I do to deserve a communication intern?" He inspected both wrists and said, "I told you I wanted a wrist communicator and here I am talking to my foot. If the powers-that-be wanted this done right they …"

Sola, safe on her home planet, interrupted, "Hold on mister. You have to look like an English speaking foreigner (a *gringo*) so I made you tall and white. Also, you must dress like the expats living in Merida, but how could I know what they wear? They're from the North America so they could dress like Eskimos or Apache Indians for all I know. Improvise, I say. Over and…"

"Stay on the wavelength you fool. It gets worse. What's the function of this dangling appendage? It gets in the way when I bend over to communicate."

"And, you accuse me of not doing my research? The function of the appendage is to micturate and procreate," Sola said.

"It's flapping against my knees you idiot. I could empty my human bladder just as well with a compact appendage."

"Did you forget about procreation?" Sola asked. "My data sources tell me that for effective impregnation, the proliferation app must penetrate the female receptacle. "

His gringo face burned red with anger, "Put it where you say? That's it. Bring me home. This is just too bizarre."

"I won't bring you home and appear incompetent to my superiors," she said. "I know I'm a green intern, but I have my pride. No, I won't do it. Find a willing receptacle and make a deposit."

"And, my young ignorant, what exactly am I depositing?"

"Spermatozoa I think. I'll get back to you."

With his frame folded over to communicate with his ankle, the moonlight reflected off his upturned backside. What looked like a translucent globe floating about four feet off the ground caught the amused attention of Valerie Pickles of the Pickled Onion, a hotel and restaurant down the road in Santa Elena. Valerie held a wait-and-see stoicism about the end of the world and a live-and-let-live attitude about the characters invading the serenity of the Yucatan.

Her chuckle changed to a gasp as the startled Chars4 bolted upright and spun to face his intruder.

Although he attempted a casual smile, Valerie saw the fear and confusion in his eyes, "Which group are you with? Can I help you find them?"

"I am not with a group," he replied. "I am a social scientist from France. The name is Chars4. If you can help me, I do need a covering for this body. Also, I need to make my way to Merida, Yucatan to join the Merida English Library."

"Happy to meet you Chars Four. I don't recognize Four as a French surname. Is it Defour?"

Vowing to report Sola's incompetence and to always introduce himself as Chars, he said, "You can call me Chars."

He doesn't seem like a pervert. He's making no attempts to cover his penis, yet he doesn't display it either. Valerie noted that if Chars is any indication, Frenchmen are more endowed than their British counterparts. Showing her live-and-let-live attitude but acknowledging the need for at least a legal pretense

[129]

of modesty, Valerie slid her red and silver *rebozo* (a Mexican shawl) from her shoulders and tied it around his waist. After inspecting the coverage, she had to tug the rebozo lower on his hips to conceal his appendage.

Grateful for Valerie's kindness, he followed her to the Pickled Onion, where end-of- the- world tourists had stuffed themselves into her hotel like stuffed olives crammed into a jar. She gave him a worn pair of jeans, a faded blue polo, and well-traveled flip flops — all left by a hotel guest. Valerie directed Chars to a poolside hammock, saying she could drive him to Merida in the morning.

∞

The extraterrestrial advance team, saying they were from France, had reserved a *casita* (a small guest house) for Chars4 at the Los Arcos B&B, on Calle 66 around the corner from the Merida English Library. Dave Reed, the owner, showed the lanky foreigner the backpack and clothes the team had left for him, and handed him an envelope of Mexican currency. Because Interpol is located in Paris, Dave assumed his guest must be an agent.

"Welcome to Merida," said Dave. "You look pale as a new sheet; I'd slather on some sunscreen right away. By the way, the library is hosting a cocktail party tonight. You can meet other English speakers if you like."

After Dave had left the room to tend to other guests, Chars4 parked himself on the edge of the bed, crossing his left leg over his right knee to better access his ankle communication implant. No more waving his behind to the heavens.

He spoke without the customary pleasantries, "Sola, tell the Powers that I am ready. Confirm that my assignment is two-fold: first, transport the Roswell offspring and second, impregnate a few human females who are born of human parents. Do the group members know they are the offspring of the Roswell survivors who mated with humans?"

"They were never intended to know," answered Sola.

"They weren't? So, how can they know why they are all directed to assemble in Merida at the Merida English Library?"

Sola replied, "They don't know."

"They don't? Whatever, I will need to evaluate their adjustment before I tell them what they all have in common, why they all felt compelled to relocate in Merida. You should have given me better data. If I get found out, life on Earth will never be the same."

"Don't be so dramatic," she said.

"You are new to this, little girl. Mark my words. Humans will shoot nuclear arms blindly into outer space and then we'll have a planetary disaster. These humans are clueless about the traffic just outside their awareness."

Ignoring his dismissive comments Sola said, "Remember, you must get the Roswell offspring back here by the next full moon. That's in six days. Whatever you do, do not get caught. Remember the time you were almost captured by the military in Brazil? You refused a human body disguise and terrified the locals. I don't know how much longer we can cover up your negligence."

"No one asked for your analysis, Missy."

Stifling a chuckle, Sola said, "By the way, the deposit you asked about is spermatozoa. Sorry."

"It's okay; I've become an admirer of this multitasking appendage."

"I'm envious," she said.

The library garden stood lush with aromatic tropical plants while the twinkling lights adorning the trees created a contented glow over the buzz of English chatter. How could he identify the geriatric offspring from the Roswell Incident? Chars4 sat on a bench near the back wall of the garden, pretending to remove a stone from his sandal.

"Sola, they're all ancient and I can't identify the accents. But, when I get within three feet, the brain wave exchange begins and I do feel a pull toward certain individuals."

"No brainer, Chars4. You will feel a connection with the parts of the brain that are wired to your frequency. Of course, they are old. Our people crashed in 1947, so depending on how long it took them to adapt and procreate…"

"So my Roswell kiddos are around sixty-five and maybe a little younger? Are you sure they are programmed to assemble at the library this year, before the next full moon?"

"Yes, of course. It is built into their DNA," Sola responded.

Chars4 ended the communication when he felt a hand on his shoulder.

"Hi, I'm Dan Karnes, president of the library. It's always nice to see a new face. Come, meet some people." Dan felt a strange kinship with this too tall and too pale gringo. Chars4 felt the same bond and in his human heart, knew he had been welcomed by the first member of his group. He stood ready to discover the rest of his Roswell offspring people.

To everyone he met, he introduced himself as Chars, a social scientist from France doing a study on what attracts foreigners to the Yucatan. He met with more than 60 people, who, one way or another said they retired to the Yucatan because they felt they were drawn here.

With Dan's help, he spoke with everyone with whom he felt a brainwave exchange. Although he felt an affinity toward the project people and was warmed by their interest in him, he worried about being detected. He pledged not to repeat the Brazilian experience. Not that any of that fiasco was his fault. He did learn, however that a human disguise is mandatory despite its inconvenience. After the party, he returned to his casita to report his progress.

"Sola," he said, "it is as if they already knew. They knew that I knew and I knew that they knew I knew."

"Stifle the linguistic showoff and tell me what happened when you told them of our mission—you know—to return them to the homeland of their alien parent."

"Some asked about assisted living facilities, but other than that they seemed eager to sign up for the voyage. Many said they felt misplaced their entire lives and have always searched for a place in which they felt at home."

Sola asked, "How did you handle the ones who were not from your group?"

"Some just laughed thinking it was either an end-of-the-world joke or that I was left over from the collection of weirdos at Uxmal. I did find the Roswell offspring and most agreed to return. That takes care of part one of this assignment. Part two, the procreation caper turns out to be more troublesome."

Sola's voice crackled over the communicator, "I hope you crafted a plan."

"I managed to find females in this library group who were not drawn here and who are not Roswell offspring. Maybe them?"

"Once more, here are your procreation criteria: No Roswell offspring, they must be adult human females and not in menopause."

"Oh crap, they are all menopausal age, but some appealing young Mexican college students do frequent the library."

[133]

"Absolutely not. This is a longitudinal study and you must be exact. Only subjects from the United States and Canada are acceptable."

"Don't worry; I do have a Plan B. The Centro house tour is tomorrow afternoon. I'm sure I'll find some non-menopausal females from north of the border to impregnate."

At the house tour, Chars4 spotted a sparkly-eyed, twenty-something with sandy blond hair and a musical Texas drawl. His appendage sat up and took notice. From house-to- house he hounded her; his proposals of impregnation growing more desperate and insistent. If only he had more time. Upset and frightened, she complained to the house tour organizers who in turn called the authorities. As he pursued the lovely up Calle 53, a speeding black-on-black pickup truck veered onto the sidewalk, screeched to a stop and blocked his path. Two of the six officers jumped from the vehicle, grabbed him, slapped on handcuffs and threw him on the steel bed of the patrol truck. The other four watched with their AK 47's aimed at his forehead, hoping for a show of resistance.

∞

Chars4 sat on his cot in a 4x8 holding cell, the iron bars casting a striped shadow across his dejected form.

Sola was not sympathetic. "I don't know what to tell you. You've messed up this mission for the both of us. I bet the military is on its way. If you... "

"It's your fault," Chars4 interrupted, "Why didn't you brief me on seduction techniques for the human female?"

"That wasn't my job, mister senior operative who knows everything about women."

"I do know everything about our women, but not yet for humanoids."

"I'm going to put in my report that you are an interplanetary misogynist."

"Who cares? Just get me out of here."

"I can't, you are on your own, little mister."

※

Dan, the library president, called a meeting of a few members of the Roswell offspring group to see how they might secure his release. They didn't want anything, even his apparent sex perversion, to hinder their return to the homeland of their non-human parent. They met with the young woman he was chasing and gave her a story that he was socially inept and perhaps IQ challenged. She withdrew her complaint and the officials released Chars4 to Dan's custody. With Dan now a trusted friend, the former convict divulged the procreation part of his mission.

"Dan, my new friend, I cannot return home unless I impregnate at least three women from north of the border. Getting this conjoint coitus accomplished before we leave next week is impossible. Besides my procreation sensor is all out of whack. It's supposed to tingle when a viable candidate is in the range, but so far, it's only tingled for one woman and that tingle landed me in jail."

Dan was sympathetic, "I'm sorry this is happening to you Chars. You might have to return without meeting your impregnation goals."

The frustrated alien lowered his eyelids, a human sign of surrender, and said, "You may be right, Dan."

※

They met at 7 pm in the Nun's Quadrangle at Uxmal, on the evening of the full moon on 27th of December, 2012, just six days after his arrival. Forty-five of the original sixty chose to return with Chars4. The other fifteen assembled to bid them farewell. Others, who lived close by, milled around, waiting to see if the rumors were true. Would ascension happen this very night? Valerie Pickles from the nearby Pickled Onion was saying goodbye to friends who were leaving.

Chars4 beckoned the travelers to move closer to him, "Everyone, gather around me and squeeze together. We'll try to get the entire group to ascend at the same time."

Ignoring the persistent and intensifying tingle from his ankle communicator, he said, "Before we head into transport phase, I shall explain the path of wormholes that will make up our journey. First…"

The ankle tingle, now Taser strength, commanded his attention, "Sola, I don't have time for this. We are about to ascend."

Sola's voice crackled over the communication device as the lunar frequencies readied for transport, "Step aside Chars4," she said. "You will not return until you complete your mission of procreation."

Exasperated with her affected authoritarian attitude he said, "Says who, Missy?"

Sola's smirk of a voice left the frequency and the cold booming voice of his superior spilled out over the communication device like an icy avalanche.

"You will not come home," the voice said, "until you complete your mission. You have until the summer solstice. Six months, that's all, no more. If I hear that you have done anything to call military attention to your activities, you will be retired."

"Please," Chars4 pleaded. "If only I could transfer to the U.S. or Canada. That's where the target females are located."

"You will stay in Mexico until you complete your assignment." His superior closed the frequency and left him no option but to step aside as the group ascended.

Precisely at 7:15 pm, witnesses heard the tinkling of a million tiny crystal bells accompanying a hummingbird vibration of fuchsia twinkles and a heady scent of night blooming jasmine. A sigh of blissful empathy from the remaining fifteen was the last sound the voyagers heard. The onlookers watched in awe as the traveler's bodies became increasingly translucent. As the moonlight shone through their images, their forms faded and in less than thirty seconds, vanished. Cheers of celebration from the onlookers echoed throughout the silence of Uxmal as tears of rapture sprang from their eyes. They were gone. The fragrance of jasmine lingered and the compound filled with quiet and moonlight, just like any Yucatan night.

The discarded extraterrestrial sat on the ground, apart from the onlookers. They watched as he persistently punched his ankle, calling out for someone to listen, for someone, anyone to help him. No answer.

A few of the remaining group members beckoned Chars4 to join them as they made their way back to the chartered bus. He waved them off with a tired gesture. "Oh, come on Chars," one said, "We're going on to Cancun. I know you'll have fun. Lots of women there and we all know how much you like the ladies."

In one leap, Chars4 kissed Valerie on the cheek, grabbed his backpack and landed on the bus. Valerie shook her head as she imagined the next six months of the alien sex addict attempting to combine his genetic material with that of unsuspecting young women in Cancun. She saw only two possibilities for him: arrest and imprisonment or death from non-stop sex.

News of Chars4 and his indiscriminate seed spreading traveled to Merida. Just before Valentine's Day, Valerie heard that he was to be featured in a T.V. special filmed in Cancun. Worried that he had found his way to "America's Most Wanted, "Valerie joined the remainder of the project people at the library to watch on the big screen T.V.

The show opened, not with a list of the FBI's most wanted, but with a bevy of bikinied beauties cavorting in the sun and sand against a backdrop of a tranquil Caribbean blue sea. The camera zoomed to Chars4 sporting a grin as broad as a barracuda's and an electric blue Speedo that barely accommodated his appendage. The group delighted in finding him in the center of an assembly of topless bathing beauties. However, they were all astonished to hear him introduced as the new on-air talent for the popular T.V. series, "Girls Gone Wild."

CHERIE PITTILLO

How Not to Social Network

Social Flycatcher
Social Flycatcher, Myiozetetes similis, luis gregario (Spanish),
x takay (Mayan)

Although one of the attractions of living in Merida is the friendliness of the people, unfortunately this doesn't apply to the largest family of birds in the world, the tyrant flycatchers. Several members of this 400 plus species group of feather floggers live in the Yucatan Peninsula, but today I concentrate on the so-called Social Flycatcher.

This species ranges from Mexico to Peru and Northern Argentina. I often see or hear the noisy chattering in my backyard, the many parks of Merida, and on most birding trips in the Yucatan.

With its zebra-striped head adorning a white throat and vivid yellow vest, the adult resembles two other common tyrant flycatchers here, the Boat-billed Kiskadee and the Great Kiskadee. Both are larger and have bigger bills while the Great Kiskadee has rusty-colored wing margins.

If I placed one in my hand, it would stretch from the base of my palm to the tip of my middle finger about seven inches. Why is this smallish bird called a tyrant flycatcher? One universal characteristic is its aggression. Another is its typical feeding behavior of sitting on a perch where it then sallies forth to catch an insect in the air. The Social Flycatcher also devours spiders, seeds, fruits, and even tadpoles.

Now imagine a White-winged Dove and several smaller Ruddy Ground-Doves as they settle on utility lines to preen, relax, signal to mate, and mate. Next, one Social Flycatcher joins them.

Does the less-than-one ounce terrorist relax? No. Each Ruddy Ground-Dove raises a wing or two perhaps to scare this intruder. That doesn't work. The intimidator pursues all of them.

Here is the final outcome: Social Flycatcher 5, Doves 0. So much for that social networking ability.

I hereby rename this species the Anti-social Flycatcher because I see it chase every species that comes near it whether parrot or *paloma* (dove). Okay, it does stay paired all year, and its family is a social group that stays together until just after breeding season. I'll give it that much sociability.

Go outdoors and discover another social network in the animal kingdom this week.

DISCLAIMER: *References do not agree on information about this species. Here are my resources: A Guide to the Birds of Mexico and Northern Central America, Birds and Reserves of the Yucatan Peninsula, National Geographic Field Guide to the Birds of North America, A Guide to the Birds of Costa Rica, Kaufman Field Guide to Birds of North America, and* http://macaulaylibrary.org *a website from Cornell Lab of Ornithology*

First published in The Yucatan Times, Backyard Birding in Merida, Yucatan and Beyond

THERESA DIAZ GRAY

Frances and the False Friends

A short language lesson before we begin our tale.

False cognates, also known as the false friends, are the mean girls of the language world. They delight in tripping us up. They are words that appear to be cognates but aren't.

Cognates are words that have the same linguistic roots and meaning. For example, abnormal is written the same way in both Spanish and English, just pronounced a little differently, so is actor. Other words are close enough so you can easily guess– attention – atención, period – periodo, and zodiac – zodíaco.

Frances eats lunch:
Frances liked to think of herself as adventurous, her older sister always said that Frances lacked impulse control and was prone to making rash decisions. Frances thought that Beulah was just jealous. Beulah wouldn't recognize spontaneity if it bit her, it took big sister three days to plan a shopping trip to the nearest big city.

Frances's announcement of her plan to move to Mexico had the whole family rolling their eyes, an intervention was even orchestrated by big sis! Good thing that she didn't admit to having bought a house, sight unseen, over the internet in Merida. Even Frances was having doubts about the wisdom of that particular proposition, but who could resist buying a house for thirty eight thousand dollars even if it wasn't quite livable yet.

Sitting at the little neighborhood restaurant just down the street from her rental, she thought back on how well she had handled Beulah's ploy to keep her from her goal of retiring early and living a life of ease south of the border.

"You don't even speak Spanish, and the food is so spicy! What will you eat?" Mama put ketchup on spaghetti because marinara was too exotic. Onions were okay, but she drew the line at garlic. Food was always a big concern with Mama.

"Yes, I do speak Spanish, Mama. I took a semester at the city college. When I went to Mexico on vacation everyone in Cancun and Playa del Carmen spoke English, Merida won't be any different." Frances deftly avoided the food issue.

Mama didn't really need to worry, Frances had a plan to deal with the few people who didn't speak English, and she would simply add an "A" or an "O" to the end of the words. She had discovered English and Spanish had scads of cognates.

The questions about crime and kidnappings were dealt with by Frances passing out fact sheets that she had prepared. In bold letters she had printed across the top, Merida is one of the safest cities in Mexico.

All reminiscing aside, she was here now, and hungry to boot.

The next door neighbors' *cocina economica* was open. The Rodriguez family created a dining space by cramming six red plastic Coca Cola tables under their carport. All morning the smell of *comida tipica* flowed down the street. Frances checked out the blackboard which boasted a couple of daily dishes all costing about three bucks. She had learned that the breaded pork was always good and plain, so she ordered that.

Laydi, the cook's daughter, bumped open the screen door, and served Frances her food with a flourish. Frances looked suspiciously at what appeared to be a small ripe bell pepper decorating her plate. Time to haul out the Spanish, "*¿Es caliente?*" she asked. She added in English to make sure, "Is it hot?"

What was this French woman thinking? She probably had seen too many Chilies TV commercials with their sizzling Tex-Mex fajita platters. Laydi had left the plate cooling on the counter until it reached room temperature in the traditional Yucatecan manner. "*No caliente, comida caliente no es sano.*" Everyone knows that hot food is not healthy to eat.

Ah ha! A cognate, sane, so Laydi didn't like spicy food either! Frances took a small nibble of the pretty red pepper, no problem. Confidently, she popped the whole thing into her mouth. Sweat broke out on her forehead, her ears not only felt red hot, they actually turned maroon. Laydi's eyes got huge, she ran inside yelling, "*¡La Francesa se enchiló!*" and returned in a flash with a huge spoon of sugar for Frances to eat. Meanwhile, the gentleman at the next table offered his coke, saying in English "Drink this it will help cut the heat." His companion, said, "No eat some tortillas that will help." Eventually, the infernal burning in her mouth stopped.

"Thank you," she said to her helpers.

"Oh, you speak English, I thought Laydi said that you're French." the woman answered.

"I have no idea where she got that idea." Frances replied, "My name is Frances Ford. I introduced myself the first day but got a really confusing answer from Laydi."

Frances repeated that conversation to her new friends. "Buenos dias, soy Frances." I said in my best Spanish.

"*Yo soy Yucateca, me llamo Laydi ¿y tú?* (I am Yucatecan, my name is Laydi, and you?)" was Laydi's puzzling reply. Wasn't it obvious that Frances was an American? Why did Laydi tell her that she was Yucatecan?

"Pleased to meet you Frances, I am Ed and my wife is Sherry. I speak a tiny bit of Spanish but Sherry is pretty fluent."

Sherry took over the conversation. "*Francés* means French in Spanish, so Laydi thought that you were telling her that you are French. By the way, a word that you might want to use instead of *caliente* is *picante*. When you asked, Laydi if the food was hot, she thought you were asking about the temperature of the plate. Yucatecans believe that food should be eaten at room temperature to be healthy. Picante means spicy hot, like in the habanero chile you so daringly ate."

Frances goes shopping:

Frances wished that she had Sherry and her superior language skills with her when she went to the small neighborhood store to buy some clothesline. The owner of the shop, Gordon, was a chubby cheerful man but seriously lacking in imagination when it came to deciphering what Frances wanted. She had found his store by asking Laydi, who said, "El Gordón will have you needs." Laydi liked to practice her English even if it was a bit fractured. Frances thought that using *el* that way was charming, similar to how her Celtic friends referred to The O'Neil.

"*Ropa por favor, Gordón.*" Frances said. The store owner, squinted at her and shrugged his mighty shoulders. He had dealt often enough with the French lady to know that she never really wanted what she was asking for. Even la francesa should know that you don't buy clothing at a hardware store. He sighed and resigned himself to playing a guessing game.

"*No hay. Tienes que ir al centro.*" Frances understood that much Spanish, she'd learned that *no hay* meant there isn't any, even if there was some, and of course she knew that centro meant downtown. No hay seemed to be the automatic response to her requests.

She was determined to not leave the store without some rope. "Sí hay," she insisted, "quiero pinas y ropa" while making pinching motions.

"*¿Pinzas, pinzas de ropa?*" ah ha, we were finally getting somewhere, she wants clothespins! Unless she wanted pineapples, but she said pina not piña. He decided to try the clothespins first. He rooted around under the counter. He produced a dusty package of clothesline and bright pink plastic clothespins and presented it with a flourish. *"Pinzas y soga. No hay solo pinzas."* He hoped that she would buy the whole package, though he was willing to just sell the clothespins, he even would sell her one clothespin if it would get her out of his store.

"See, I told you there was ropa!" Frances, spoke in English in her excitement at finally getting what she wanted. She recovered enough to ask how much. As she counted out the coins, she smiled and said, "Gracias, Gordón."

Later when Frances was telling her story to Sherry over coffee, Sherry chuckled and said, "Poor Don Felix, he really doesn't have much experience dealing with non-Spanish speakers. I'm glad you were able to finally get some line."

"I didn't go to see this Don person, I went to el Gordón." answered Frances, feeling clever to have remembered adding the *el*.

Sherry was glad she had already set down her cup, she barely choked out the words "El Gordón you called him Gordón?"

After she caught her breath she continued, "Don is an honorific, his real name is Felix. Don Felix is the owner of the store. El gordón means the really fat guy. I imagine he was much heavier when he was younger." Frances was horrified, she had been calling that nice man, Fatso.

Frances goes to a party:
Sherry convinced Frances to take Spanish lessons when she found that she wasn't absorbing Spanish as quickly as she thought that she should. Frances blamed the Yucatecan accent, and all those Maya words. She had gotten an A in both of her semesters of Spanish after all, so the problem wasn't her at all. She had insisted in being put in the intermediate class over her teacher's objections. Now her teacher was having all the students over for a cocktail party to practice their language skills with non-English speakers.

The class had a list of things that they were to accomplish at the party, the more items crossed off the list the better their grade.

1. Talk to at least three non-classmates in Spanish.

2. Meet someone new and introduce the teacher to them. (Frances felt that should count as two separate items.)

3. Ask about the latest movie.

4. Talk about the weather.

Frances was stunned by the beautiful mid-century modern house, she never even considered living in one of the older *colonias* (neighborhoods). She wanted high ceilings and thick walls of a colonial house in centro but this house was also huge and airy.

"*Permítame presentarme, me llamo* Frances Ford." Her teacher had convinced her that it would be less confusing if she told people her name is Frances rather than saying that she was Frances. This seemed like the perfect time to use the phrase. Frances felt very sure of herself as she introduced herself to the handsome youngster standing in the corner sipping the ubiquitous Coca Cola.

"Mucho gusto, soy Julio Jiménez." Julio smiled shyly, he had never spoken to a foreigner before.

What to say next? Time to check item number four off her list. The weather is always a safe topic. "*Soy calient ¿estas caliente tambien?*" Frances remarked on how hot she felt as she waved her fragrant sandalwood fan in front of her face in an unconsciously flirtatious manner. Julio looked like he was having a hot flash as he turned beet red, almost spilling his drink. What do you say when someone tells you that they are aroused and want to know if you are too?

Just then Frances's teacher, Maria Elena happened to walk by. Frances smiled. Another item to cross off her list. "Maria Elena, permita me introducerle a Julio." Julio blanched and took a gulp of his soda, he had heard that Americans had loose morals but the lady couldn't possibly be suggesting a threesome?

Quickly, Maria Elena offered up some rapid fire Spanish, too fast for Frances to understand. Turning to Frances, she explained, "Frances, in Spanish, the word, *introducir*, means to place one object inside another. The correct word is *presentar*. Also we say have heat, not that we are hot, I'll explain that later."

Frances gulped, "*Soy muy embarazada, perdóname.*" Frances looked too old to be pregnant but there had been that woman in Italy, Julio decided that being polite is always the best option and congratulated Frances, "*Felicidades*". Maria Elena silently decided that her next lesson plan would definitely be about false cognates and excused herself as she went off in search of a drink.

Frances gets her haircut:

One of the things Frances really loved about living in Mexico was that everyone delivered. When she painted the house, the guy from Comex loaded her paint on a dolly and walked the four blocks to her house. When she didn't feel like cooking, *Big Chicken* delivered chicken, soggy spaghetti, and rice to her door via motorcycle. Her new coffee guy, Juan Carlos, drove a battered VW bug to make his deliveries. The previous coffee vendor used a bicycle but he went on vacation for two weeks at Easter without saying a word. He always went on vacation for Semana Santa he explained when he ran into Frances, but she had already changed coffee providers and Juan Carlos seemed more reliable, plus his coffee was better. Now she was going to try something totally new, someone was coming to cut her hair at her house!

Silvia, the manicurist, who also came to her house, convinced Frances to try her sister Dulce's haircutting service. Silvia's hair always looked so good, Frances was willing to try.

Dulce arrived on time. They went out into the yard to work under the sour orange tree where Frances had set out a plastic chair and table. Best to start with just a trim, "*Chiquito corto, por favor.*"

Dulce smiled, she loved it when her clients wanted a bold new look. Silvia was right, Frances did speak enough Spanish, what a relief! The phrasing was odd, short, please small, but the intent was clear. She knew just the perfect pixie cut, but just to be sure she held her fingers apart about an inch. Frances nodded her head enthusiastically.

Frances relaxed as Dulce cut her hair. They chatted. Frances started to worry when she realized that there was a lot of hair littering the ground. After removing the plastic cape, sweeping the stray hairs away, Dulce presented Frances with a hand mirror.

Frances was stunned. A different woman stared back at her, short pixie cut making her eyes look huge.

Frances decided that her new look was a metaphor for her life in Mexico. Unexpected, but not necessarily bad. She did however, vow to really, really, work on her Spanish.

CHERIE PITTILLO

Things that Make Me Smile in Merida

- a Volkswagen driving through an intersection pulling a grocery cart as a small trailer
- the name of a local radio station, KISS FM, because "KISS" sounds like the Mayan word for "fart"
- when my husband first saw the sign for OXXO, an abundant convenience store, he translated it as "Oh, look, it's Hugs and Kisses!"
- how we are never invisible here:
  - when we walk into or leave a restaurant, Yucatecans greet us and wish us to have a good meal
  - whether we or anyone enters a doctor's, dentist's, or veterinarian's office, Yucatecans in the waiting room greet us
  - how people of any age, including teenagers, smile and greet as I walk down the street
  - how helpful any Yucatecan tries to be

- the lead surgeon for my husband's total knee replacement came to our home twice in two weeks after the surgery
- we never have to pump gasoline because all stations are full service
- the variety of sounds from whistles, bells, and mooing cow to announce the different door-to-door vendors such as knife-sharpening or fermented pineapples or especially the milk and cheese delivery
- the only turquoise-painted, wooden front door in our block
- we live in Centro with more than a million people, yet our backyard is quiet and peaceful
- embedded reflectors in the middle of the roads are called "ojos de gatos"…cat eyes

GWEN LANE

Crickets and Cheese Please

Some people around the world appreciate onions, garlic, chili and lime sautéed in virgin olive oil, served on a bed of rice with slightly toasted and well-seasoned insects. I can't move past the creep factor.

One hot spring day while my mother and her friend visited, we meandered around the Oaxaca food and handicraft fair at Peace Park.

We viewed the scarves, jewelry, bright-colored clothing, handicrafts and pottery. A woodsy smoked scent enticed us to the food area.

After review of the menu we ordered the sampler platter of different Oaxaca foods: cheese, chocolate, black beans, moles and meats.

I enjoy trying new foods and like many of them. Hubby, served a little of everything on each plate.

"What's this?" I ask.

"*Chapulines frito*." he replied, as my eyes became fixated on

pieces that looked like legs and bug heads.
"What's that?" Mom asks.
"Crickets!" I cringed, "Fried grasshoppers."
> You may like them, you will see.
> You may like them, follow me.

Our waiter explained that they contain a lot of protein and have been eaten in Oaxaca since prehistoric time. First I listened in Spanish while the waiter told how they collected them in a net in the fields, cleaned and either fry or toast them on a *comal* with chili, lime and garlic. You can eat them solo or on a tostada, taco or guacamole. Then I endured the story again while Hubby explained in English for our guests.

My dining companions managed to put a small portion in their mouths. They agreed the *chapulines* crunched and tasted spicy and well-seasoned but I noticed no forks moved to the mouth for a second taste.

"Why don't you want to even try them? Usually you enjoy trying new and different things." My mother tried appealing to my adventuresome side.

> I could not, would not try a bite.
> I cannot, will not taste this sight.

I could barely contain my laughter and proceeded to tell my story from last summer.

Our girls' bedroom overlooks the garden and patio and at night they heard cricket noises. Sometimes the girls woke me up in the middle of the night and told me the crickets sounded so loud they couldn't sleep. I went on a cricket hunt; turned off lights, closed quietly in on a sound, searched behind curtains, under tables and behind closets – flashlight in one hand, spray in the other.

CRICKETS AND CHEESE PLEASE

The noise stopped for a moment and I wanted to claim victory – only to hear another or maybe the same chirp-chirp.

> I'm going on a cricket hunt, I'm not afraid,
> Got my flashlight, got my spray.

At first I thought only a few crickets had strayed, but after several weeks, those elusive critters began to invade my dreams. Bigger chirps seemed to be calling smaller chirps.

One night I saw several black bugs the size of large ants crawling around the floor of the girls' bedroom. I watched them march towards a louder chirp that appeared to be waiting for them at an exit that led to the patio only to be trapped at the new threshold we installed to keep the cool air in. There they became easy prey for my heavy foot.

Ants are a common nuisance in Yucatan. They range in size from a quarter of an inch long with large heads and bodies to the barely visible. I realized after living here several months the littlest ones walked up arms and legs without being detected by the eye but their bite felt like small needle pokes.

In Oaxaca, at the beginning of the rainy season, a bug appears called *chicatanas*. They look like large ants with wings. They are toasted, ground up and prepared in salsas. But, I digress.

I narrowed the hunt to a canvas box containing papers and books. But when I searched the box I found no crickets. Perplexed, I repacked it and returned it to the room. That very night I heard chirping noises from the canvas box again. I moved it outside, where crickets belong.

I became obsessed with finding where those crickets had set up their base. The next morning I examined the canvas box more closely, removing each paper, each book, and each toy until I noticed a rectangular wooden puzzle box, eight inches by six inches, with a sliding door. Inside I remembered there were four compartments, holding pieces for four different jigsaw puzzles.

The sliding wooden door was open about half inch, and covered with a suspicious fuzz and lint. Aha! I was onto something, so I prepared for what I hoped would be the final search and destroy mission. I grabbed one of my shoes, my weapon of convenience and carefully carried the wooden box outside to a pathway that led to the pool.

I had not prepared well for what happened next. When I began to open the box hundreds of crawling crickets scrambled to vacate, scurrying in all directions seeking safe shelter somewhere.

Bam, bam, bam, I used the shoe in my hand to squish the invading mob as quickly as I could before they hid in the garden. Bam, bam I hit the ones crawling up the wall.

When I tried to get close enough to close the box, big black bugs crawled up my bare arms and legs, using my feet as a rampart. I retreated and shook them off.

I realized I had opened Pandora's Box of bugs; there was no turning back.

After a few minutes of chasing down and stomping them to black blotches on the cement, I heard Hubby behind me. "What in the world is going on out here? It sounds like practice for a dance troupe."

"I'm in battle with an army of crickets and I need reinforcements now!"

"Hold on I'll bring the heavy artillery." We had joined forces and prepared to conquer.

I continued smashing the crawly beasts as they tried to find sanctuary between my toes.

Hubby returned wielding a huge can of bug spray, "You secure the walkway and walls and I'll get the ones in the garden." He

CRICKETS AND CHEESE PLEASE

had taken over as commanding officer but it sounded like a good plan to me.

Ten minutes after the battle commenced all the bugs had left their bunker. The crawly invaders had abandoned their headquarters. We searched around for a few escapees before declaring victory.

By now curious children had to know what was going on in the garden. I explained we had found the cricket house but not to worry, we had taken care of it.

I was thankful no one had wanted to play with that puzzle box in the last month or so. Imagine the panic if those crickets had escaped, crawling over them and into all the corners of the bedroom and house. I would have been soothing nightmares for months.

But the fun was not over yet. With the typical curiosity of a seven year old, our son examined the wooden box we'd abandoned outside.

"Oooo! Mama, come look at this."

"Ooooo is right, yuck!" We all agreed. Mounds of white, slimy larvae weaved in between and pasted around the small puzzle pieces. At least what was left in the box wasn't moving.

Hubby came to the rescue again and volunteered to clean up the whole oozy mess. All watched as he bravely filled a bucket with soap and water, dunked the puzzle box and cleaned it with his bare hands. He hosed each piece of the four puzzles and laid them on the sunny concrete to dry. Then he added bleach to the bucket and let the larvae stew to oblivion.

And that is why...

> I cannot, will not
> Eat them at the fair.
> I cannot, will not
> Eat them anywhere.

UNIQUELY YUCATAN

For those wanting a more daring gastronomical experience than me, I offer the following recipe.

Prep time: 20 minutes – Cook time 10 minutes
½ kilo *chapulines*
3 cloves garlic, peeled and chopped
1 Serrano chili, seeded and diced
1 lime, cut into wedges
½ onion, chopped
½ cup oil for frying
Salt to taste

Pull the wings and legs off of each *chapaline*. Heat oil in a shallow pan and sauté garlic, chili and onions until onions are translucent. With a slotted spoon, remove and discard the onion, chili and garlic from the oil, leaving oil in the pan. Sauté the *chapalines* in the oil until they are brown and crispy. Remove the *chapalines* and drain them well on paper towels.

Sprinkle salt and squeeze lime over the top. Enjoy them as a snack or filling for tacos.

Important Tip If enjoyed in a taco, add some guacamole or *chiltomate* sauce to keep the *chapulines* in the taco.

Buen Provecho.

Parts of this story were inspired after nightly reading for many months of a favorite Dr. Seuss story.

CHERIE PITTILLO

Saltator with a Side of Greens

The Grayish Saltator
Grayish Saltator, *Saltator coerulescens*, picurero grisáceo (Spanish), tzapiim (Mayan)

The first time a Merida friend identified a songbird with the common name of the Grayish Saltator to me, I laughed. Since I'm from the southern US, "tater" is slang for "potato." Images of salt crystals sparkling on a plain, baked potato danced in my head. That may be appropriate, as "saltator" is Latin for "dancer" or "leaper." Surely, a southern chef named this bird, but, no, a Frenchman did. When he saw the bird hop on the ground, it looked too heavy to do so.

Surprise, surprise. This bird appears hefty, but it only weighs the same as a fast food hash brown, that two-ounce potato pancake. I'm beginning to see a vegetable relationship here.

In my opinion, the Grayish Saltator is the vegan of the bird world. Most sources state it eats fruits, berries, and buds. I wonder if that includes spuds buds. It may also snag slow-moving insects. After a ton of research, I found two studies done in the tropics, which discussed its diet that includes foliage and other vegetation.

What a relief! Because for several years, I've observed it munching on a variety of leaves, vines, shrubs, seeds, berries, buds, and even tender tendrils in my backyard view.

Various colors adorn the plumage. With its white, Andy Rooney-like eyebrows, white throat, grayish back and wings and belly tinged with brown, (dare I say, "Hash brown?"), the adult looks drab. A younger bird has a lemony blush on its throat and eyebrows with several olive shades on its body. But one immature sported black and white polka dot decorations.

To give you insight into this article, I researched the web, several bird books, and a paid subscription to Birds of North America by the Cornell's Lab of Ornithology. Most sources exactly copied the minimal information on Wikipedia. To my disappointment, I found little information on this common bird in the Yucatan state, which ranges from Mexico to Peru and Brazil. Its larger cousin, the Black-headed Saltator also lives here and ranges down to Panama.

Do researchers choose those species to research that are pests to humans and/or those with stunning plumage? Maybe studies do exist, and I didn't find or have access to them.

Slightly smaller than the American Robin, or here, the Clay-colored Thrush, the Grayish Saltator lives in shrubs, gardens, scrub, forest edges, and semi-open areas. For the past three months, I've seen several at a time in my neighborhood. They may be the parents with their offspring. Would their chicks be called, "tater tots?"

After I saw a saltator chase away two migrating Eastern Kingbirds, I wouldn't call this species a "couch potato." Although, I don't know the extent of its aggression, it seemed to sing a victory song. One interpretation of its song from El Salvador is ¡dichoso fui!, Spanish for "I was blessed!"

I especially enjoyed hearing its song when I had a brief stay in a hospital. Rain and clouds accentuated my visit there. When I looked out the picture window in my room, I only spotted three birds. On my departure, the rain stopped as I stepped outdoors to go to the pharmacy. I breathed in fresh air and then heard the musical notes of this songster. My face softened as I lowered my head and relaxed my shoulders. I smiled my lopsided smile to myself as I gravitated toward that sound. I wanted to see this musician. There in the tree next to the pharmacy sat this rain-soaked happiness, which continued to sing, "All is right. All will be fine."

I gave thanks.

I was blessed.

DISCLAIMER: *References do not agree on details about this species. Here are my resources: A Guide to the Birds of Mexico and Northern Central America, Birds and Reserves of the Yucatan Peninsula, A Guide to the Birds of Costa Rica, http://macaulaylibrary.org a website from Cornell Lab of Ornithology, http://avibase.bsc-eoc.org/species.jsp?lang= EN&avibaseid=47BA6FAF20A9E687&sec=wiki*

First published in The Yucatan Times, Backyard Birding in Merida, Yucatan and Beyond

MARYETTA ACKENBOM

The Ruins

Dolores watched the pedestrians and the street vendors passing in front of her hotel while she waited patiently for the tour bus to arrive. The stone bench where she sat scratched her legs where they were not covered by her bermuda-length shorts. But soon she would be sitting on the plush cushions of the air-conditioned bus.

"Chichi Lol!" she heard a small voice say, and then a little girl appeared at her knees, looking into her face with adoration, blue ribbons bobbing in her straight black hair.

A young woman ran toward the child and grabbed her arm. "*No, no, niña, ven acá!*"

"It's all right," said Dolores. "I love children."

The young woman turned away; she didn't understand. One of the ever-present street-corner hammock sellers strolled over. The woman spoke to him in a babble of Spanish. He translated for Dolores, "The child thinks you her *abuela*—her grandmother. Mother say she sorry."

The woman shook her finger in the child's face and began to scold her. The Spanish taught in her high school classes, near the surface of Dolores' mind since her arrival in Yucatan, did not sound like this. The language was not Spanish. The vendor shrugged his shoulders and walked away.

Dolores cocked her head toward the pair. She understood the strange language!

"No, Mamí, don't scold the child," she told the young mother in the same language. "Maybe I look like her Chichi. My name is Lol, too. Shas, dry your tears."

The young woman stared at Dolores and hurried off, dragging the child by the hand as the little face looked back with longing at Dolores.

"Here, lady, here is the bus," announced the tour guide. Dolores gratefully climbed aboard and settled into a seat looking out the front window. *What was that all about? How had she known what the woman was saying?*

Dolores perused the tourist folders again as the bus made its way to Chichen Itza. She had read all she could find about the Maya ruins before she left Kansas City, but a brush-up wouldn't hurt. She was a life long student, and a teacher. Studying was second nature to her.

The flat land she saw from her window was overgrown with bushes and small trees. Once in awhile she spotted a bedraggled field of henequen, the sisal plant used for making rope. She had read that the descendants of the Spanish *conquistadores* used to grow it commercially, but modern plastics forced it out of the market.

Occasionally the bus went through a village. Ancient churches and tiny thatch-roofed houses looked exactly like those pictured in the tourist brochures. Brown-skinned people walked or cycled along the road or sat in makeshift chairs in front of their houses. Stray dogs stayed out of the way of the traffic, ambling along the edge of the road in front of the buildings. Dusty town squares were filled with men in sport shirts and women in *huipiles*—the embroidered cotton dresses that were the traditional Yucatecan costume.

When the bus arrived at the ruins, the guide led Dolores and the others around the ancient piles of stone as he would a herd of cattle. Dolores followed meekly, half-listening. She soaked it all in. She only became aware of the guide when he said something foolish, or obviously wrong, but she let it pass. *Why disturb the peace of other people's vacations?*

She gazed for a long time at the great pyramid, the *Castillo* as it was named in Spanish. She sat on the ground and mused over the huge opening to the sacred *cenote*, the underground river where the ancients obtained their water. When the guide led his group to the ball court, she shuddered and turned her face away. The players in the ball games often lost their heads there.

Finally, with most of the group lagging and gasping, Dolores and the others followed the guide to the *Caracol*, named in Spanish for a snail because of the spiral stairway inside. She remembered that it was really an observatory, used to obtain extremely accurate readings of the stars, planets, the moon and the sun.

They were not allowed to climb into the top of the observatory. The way was roped off by the park officials. After giving his spiel, the guide led his little group away, without realizing that one of them was missing.

Compelled by feelings she did not understand, Dolores quietly pulled aside the rope and climbed through the rubble. The broken rock she stumbled over used to be steps. She scrambled into the top of the observatory dome where she could see sunshine through the openings.

Then darkness fell and stars appeared. Dolores heard footsteps. She recognized the step of Chan, the old temple priest. When he spied her he called, "Chichi Lol, what are you doing here? You know you've been forbidden to return here!"

She heard herself saying, in that old language which was so familiar, "Chan, you yourself told me that I was a better astronomer than all the others."

"But it's not proper, Lol. Study of the heavens is for men, not women. You defile this holy place." Chan reached the top of the stairs, smoothing out the white cotton kilt he wore.

"You know that's not true."

"It is the custom, sister. You must obey the traditions. What other way is there? Our beloved god *Cha'ac* has not sent us enough rain for many seasons. Is it because you insist on behaving like a man?"

Lol looked down at her white gown, a little dusty now after the climb to the tower, and said to Chan, "I must obey my older brother, even though I know the gods are calling me to come here."

She carefully made her way down the worn stone steps and walked to her straw-thatched hut not far away. Her mind drifted, and she imagined she heard harsh voices of many people speaking a strange language.

Lol was the best observer of the skies of her time. It was a complicated system and few could interpret the movements and predict the seasons accurately. Lol knew that Chan respected her knowledge, but he could not allow his sister to overturn thousands of years of tradition, which allowed only men to perform this priestly function. He himself, of course, was the second best astronomer.

"Tradition!" Lol spat out the word to her daughter when she arrived at her hut. "That is exactly why we live in a world turning to ruin."

THE RUINS

Sasil scooped up yams and a bit of venison from the cooking fire and passed it to her mother. "Mamí, don't be upset. Here, your dinner is ready."

"Thank you, Sasil. You have ability to see and interpret the signs, too. Don't you want to develop that power?"

"No, it's not for me. But your granddaughter Shas is ready to learn, she has seen seven rains, now. I don't understand why you want to do this, it just makes life more difficult for you and for your family, but I gladly give you permission to teach Shas if that is your desire."

"I'm afraid it's too late. All our true leaders are gone. The city is crumbling; there are even weeds and small bushes growing in the cracks of the steps of the Great Pyramid. I do so much want to lead our people back to grandeur! But I am old." Lol sighed, looking around her at the dry dusty ground, and up at the too-dry thatch forming the roof of their home. "And Cha'ac has not brought rain for the corn."

Sasil squatted beside her mother as they ate. "Mamí, why do we not have leaders now? Why did they leave?"

"No one knows for sure. Times were bad a few years before I was born. My *chichi* told me there was drought and sickness, and there was fighting among the different cities. They said even the cenotes were going dry. This, my own grandmother told me before she died. One day the king and his court were here, the next they were gone. *Chichi* said she thought they had been killed. They may have just gone south into the deep jungle to find an easier place to live, a place where *Cha'ac* smiled on them and sent them rain."

They heard running steps outside the door of the hut, and a young man burst into the clearing. "Strangers!" he cried. "There are strange white men with hair on their faces. They came in huge boats!"

[167]

"Tutul, my son, where did you hear this?" asked Lol.

The young man slid to a seat beside his mother. "Mamí, messengers just arrived from the coast. The huge boat landed there, and the people at Kam Pech drove them away, but many were killed by fire-throwers."

"It is according to the legends and the omens," said Lol. "The people from the central highlands have predicted the coming of a god with white skin."

"If they're gods, they're weak ones!" said Tutul.

"But the legends say that even though individually they are weak, they are many and they have powerful weapons. We, on the other hand, may be strong, but we are few. We will never beat them back."

Tutul accepted a helping of yams from his sister. "We must try, Mamí Lol."

"Yes, we must try, even though it means the death of us all. It is too late to teach little Shas to be a strong leader."

Dolores climbed down from the dome of the Caracol and hurried to catch up with her tour group. Daylight had come again. On the way back to Merida in the bus, she pondered her experience, and decided that it was much more than a dream.

The next morning, Dolores again sat on the bench near the door of the hotel, resting before going to her room and watching the people pass by. Then, the child again ran into her arms.

"Chichi Lol!" the girl cried.

"Yes, Shas, it is I. But it is too late. Go home with your mother, now." Dolores looked up at the young mother and smiled. "Sasil, this child and other children hold the future of the race in their hands. Teach her well!"

"I will, Mamí," said Sasil. She kissed Dolores on the cheek and bade the child to do the same. Then she took Shas by the hand and led her away.

CHERIE PITTILLO

Runaway Bride

Northern Jacana
Northern Jacana, *Jacana spinosa, Jacana Norteña* (Spanish)

When I see an adult pair of birds with chicks, I usually assume those two birds were the parents. If I notice only an adult with young, I assume it's the mother. But my assumption would be wrong.

Hold onto your feathered caps, because a sexual role reversal occurs in the Yucatan Peninsula (and from Southern Texas to Western Panama and the Caribbean, too.)

Welcome to the feminist, play-girl world of the female Northern Jacana.

Larger and heavier than the male, the foot tall, female Northern Jacana, serves as overseer of a large territory with one to four males in it. Within the she-boss's playing field, every male defends his smaller turf against other males.

The amorous female mates with her selected mate-of-the-moment when he has completed their floating love nest of matted vegetation. That's a new meaning for welcome "mat".

Wonder if that was the original water bed?

She lays a clutch of three to five eggs, usually four, and then departs to carouse with others in her harem. Meanwhile each male has full parental responsibility to sit on the nest for three-four weeks and to protect and raise the chicks for several months. At least the female guards her domain against other females.

This type of breeding, termed polyandrous, is the rarest kind of mating in birds. I hereby rename the female Northern Jacana, Polyandrous Pollyanna!

Precocious chicks, called downies, can swim, dive, and feed within one-two days of hatching! Their dad leads them to food but doesn't feed them.

When I first saw a male, he had four recently hatched chicks that looked like ping pong balls tumbling on floating vegetation in search of tiny insects. How fascinating to see a chick coordinating long skinny toes at that age.

As a chick matures, yellow flight feathers adorn it like the adult. A wing adaptation, a yellow pushpin-like spur, aids in defense and combat. Another adaptation allows the young to hide submerged from predators with only their exposed bills to act as snorkels above the water's surface.

A shorebird of marshes, ponds, or even flooded pastures, the Northern Jacana, inhabits freshwater/brackish areas to feed mostly on insects found on water lilies and other floating plants. Nicknamed lily-trotters or Jesus birds, elongated toes disperse the bird's weight to walk on top of lily pads, a specialized niche where most bird species cannot walk or feed.

The Northern Jacana also dines on small fish, snails, and seeds. Sometimes it pulls up a lily pad with its bill and feet to hunt for insects. I did observe a family, less their mother of course, feeding in flooded grasses adjacent to a pond. It's as if this species lives and eats on a water bed.

Reverse your indoor role, trot out of your pad, and uncover nature's wonders.

DISCLAIMER: *References do not agree on details about this species. Here are my resources: Sal a Pajarear Yucatan, 100 Common Birds of the Yucatan Peninsula, A Guide to the Birds of Mexico and Northern Central America, Birds and Reserves of the Yucatan Peninsula, Life Histories of North American Marsh Birds, Lives of North American Birds, Southern Mexico, Birds of Costa Rica, A Neotropical Companion, Sibley Guide to Bird Life and Behaviors, http://macaulaylibrary.org Cornell Lab of Ornithology http://beautyofbirds.com/northernjacana.html, http://scienceblogs.com/tetrapodzoology/2010/07/14/spurs-blades-jacanas-lapwings/*

First published in The Yucatan Times, Backyard Birding in Merida, Yucatan and Beyond.

GWEN LANE

Yucatan Yogis

Why are you taking me off this cushy mat? I came here first. No, no, don't put me on the hard tile floor. Well, better than being outside in the rain. Don't they know by now, I am Luna, The Moon Goddess? I rule this house, upper and lower. Meow.

What are the children doing with Mom? She's a good Mom but sometimes I think she doesn't have a clue. She's trying different things to keep the children busy and off the computers this summer, by learning from new adventures.

Everyone seated on comforters on the floor, legs crossed, backs straight, wrists at the knees, eyes closed, deep breaths. Watching them makes me want to take a nap, which I had in mind before they kicked me off those blankets. Apparently, they don't have enough yoga mats and bedding has been used to soften the floor. Wish I had one.

Raising the upper torso and breathing deep, that doesn't look so hard. I think I dozed off for a moment. Kneeling, hands pressed back against the ankles, I could do that one, if only I had knees.

Oh bother, here comes that meddlesome mutt. Who let her in here? The little buttinski has to have her nose in everything. Hey, how come she gets to sit on the mat? Well, she's more like jumping and running.

They call her Star, she thinks she's the defender of the house and inspector of all who enter, but Mom calls her "doggie" a lot. Mom hasn't realized I'm Luna, Moon Goddess, and dares to address me simply as "the cat". If she can't beckon me with my proper name, she could at least bow and call me, Miss Kitty.

Star and I have lived here together for a year and a half. They adopted Star from the shelter when she was seven months old. And it shows; she still has some street habits.

I arrived two months later, a tiny kitten of 6 weeks. I don't know why my kitty Mama died when I was two weeks old. Some nice person took me to a local vet's office and asked them to find me a good home.

Now Star licks faces and walks all over their backs. She wags her stupid, out-of-control tail and smells and licks their feet. Her always wagging tail beats rapidly back and forth against the legs of the girl like a drum calling you to join in the festivities. Sometimes she moves her tail so fast her butt shakes. I still can't figure out why she adores the humans so much.

Finally, Mom tells the boy to get his dog under control. He welcomes this so he doesn't have to do yoga. Mom realizes this and takes over care of Star and tries to give her a crash course on doggy manners. Silly humans, don't they know the dog thinks the only reason they are on the ground is to play with her, of course? The dog appears quick to learn some things but social skills still challenge her.

I think the first yoga class went well. I always call any gathering where I can nap, a success.

Day 4

Oh my, it keeps getting better. Today the 84 year old Grandma joined us. While doing the lotus position in preparation for the next *asana*, Sanskrit for pose or to be established, three things happened rapidly; Grandma tooted, long and loud, the dog howled, and everyone wished Mom had not fed beans and cauliflower for lunch. Grandma might have been the first but not the only one. Star and I didn't mind the malodorous odors. Mom turned the fans on high and everyone laughed until their sides hurt. I don't know if they got more exercise from the yoga or laughing.

Returning to the yoga, lying on the back, legs pulled up to waist; turn slowly to one side and then the other. I would show you I could do that but, no one is paying attention to me. No way, I can't do any standing yoga on one leg. Who do they think I am? The Ninja Cat in Boots. They don't know of my trilingual abilities, I pretend to only understand animal lingo. Then when I ignore them they think I'm a dumb cat and don't understand.

I think I'll take a nap, then if I feel like it, a bath or maybe nap again.

I wish someone would control that overly excited perky pooch. The room is quiet and peaceful and right in the middle of my moment, the dog sits on the head of one of the girls while she lies face down. Not hard, but polite with her tail tucked to one side with front paws hanging. The girl called for help, all saw the seated dog and laughed so hard they completely forgot about the next two exercises. If she could cross her legs, she might have a lotus position for dogs.

How are these humans ever going to get enlightened?

Day 12

Maybe there is something to this yoga. I definitely feel calmer, more relaxed, refreshed, in tune with nature. Did I mention I challenged a mouse to the death the other night? But, truthfully, I didn't enjoy it as much as I used to.

Sometimes this yoga stuff makes me yawn, which I heard is a yoga asana, also called the lion's breath. Yup, that's me, the lion's breath Luna. I think I'm becoming a more accepting, tolerant and friendly feline. I'm also sleeping better and have more patience with that pathetic pooch and those hard-to-please humans; most cats won't even try to please them. I wish yoga would calm that dog down.

When I think that clumsy canine couldn't cause any more problems, she manages to prove me wrong. The humans are seated on the floor in a row with arms raised in the air, hands clasped above them and their feet extended straight. The Mexican jumping dog is on two legs, which makes her equal to Mom's elbow. In her yoga excitement and obviously doing her best to follow her version of the routine; she fell into Mom's side which knocked her off balance. Mom leaned into Grandma, who pushed on one girl who slowly descended onto her sister who tumbled onto the boy who pressed on me. Then the dog ran over to me and tried to lick my butt while my trapped head meowed to get my body out from under this pile of human dominoes. Mom tried to talk to the dog about manners again but everyone laughed so hard and missed the next three yoga asana. I have to admit, if a cat could laugh I would have, watching those silly humans tumble like leaning towers. The fun lasted till they all landed on me.

Poor dog, she seems to want to get into this yoga thing but it doesn't help her. I, on the other hand, find yoga relaxing, therapeutic, and I'm all for anything that helps me sleep better.

My favorite exercise is the deep breathing. Star told me her favorite is the doggie downward pose. I think she likes it because it gives her a chance to sniff the humans behind, lick their hands and feet, surprise them and generally make a nuisance of herself, as usual.

I thought I knew everything about cats or at least all I wanted to know. But

I didn't know that cats have a basic yoga pose named for them. It benefits your breathing, stretches muscles, stimulates gastrointestinal tract, relieves lower back pain and teaches you how to initiate movement from your center.

Let me explain how. Humans on hands and knees, animals on all four, inhale deeply, exhale. Pull abdominal muscles in and up while arching your back like a stretching cat. Head and tail bone drop down toward the floor. So simple, I think these undisciplined humans could do it.

After listening to Mom talk with the children about yoga, I think that humans stole the yoga from the animals. Many of the yoga poses come from animals. The birds have a pigeon, crow, peacock, and eagle. Other animals include the scorpion, fish, cow, camel, crocodile, and turtle. This makes perfect sense. Animals are super natural, sometimes dwelling between realms. They are not obsessed with time or status and have no ego to deal with. They just follow the rhythm of life and know where they fit in the plan.

Ancient yogis received inspiration from things around them. I don't know how inspiring these classes are, at least they get exercise. Mom's exercise seems to be helping the children do the positions correctly, watching that Grandma doesn't get hurt, and keeping that dog out of the way.

The simple cat pose doesn't challenge me anymore. Maybe I'll try the cobra, slithering in the grass, hiss, hiss, or a frog. In Mesoamerica frogs have been sacred fertility icons and symbols of death and rebirth because of their radical transformation from egg to tadpole to adult, during the life cycle. Frogs were believed to be the messengers between our physical world and the supernatural world. The frog was often carved on stone to represent the trance state of the shaman. The Ancient yogis found imitating an animal's skills uplifting and enlightening experiences and the ancient Egyptians worshipped the cat, but I'm ready to move on.

Everyone is getting stronger and able to do some of the *asana* they couldn't do a few days ago. Dissention whispers among the ranks about whether to continue with yoga after school starts. Mom thinks it would be good but only Grandma, Star and I happily agree to go on.

Mom tried to teach about the history and purpose of yoga along the way. Even I have learned some interesting things while listening and watching the video but the soothing music makes me want to take a nap.

Yoga is a Sanskrit word that implies a union or a yoking with the Supreme Spirit. It increases internal energy, self-confidence, and courage. Yoga is a practice of movements and concentration.

The point of basic yoga principles is to enrich an individual's life and spirituality, regardless of faith. Each of us is on a unique journey to fully wake up the divine spirit within. My personal favorite motto of yoga is, "Only do what you can. Honor your body". And, I might add, take a nap whenever you can.

Grandma said that doing yoga has made her feel much better and maybe she could live with us another ten or twenty years. Mom had one of those smiles that didn't tell if she felt happy or sad, probably exhausted. She's a good Mom, although sometimes clueless. I hope she takes care of me and the meddlesome mutt for many more years.

CHERIE PITTILLO

War Hero or "Rat with Wings"?

Columba livia, Rock Dove, Pigeon,
Paloma domestica (Spanish)

Walk up the steps of Merida's main square (*zocalo, plaza grande*), built on a former Maya terrace, and in the center is a raised platform within a concrete circle. In early mornings and throughout the day, this concrete pad transforms into a theater-in-the-round. Audience members can sit on park benches or in the white *confidentes* (s-shaped, side-by-side chairs) to watch the performances. Many courtship attempts occur on this stage of love. Performers strut, dance, bow, and sing softly.

Welcome to a glimpse into the world of the Rock Pigeon, commonly called pigeon.

As a male approaches a female, he "bows", puffs out his neck, coos, and dances in a circle in front of her. He high steps, stands further erect, and repeats the bowing and cooing of this "main square" dance. Sometimes he follows the females in a behavior called "driving." Also he may fan out his tail and chase her with the "tail drag" along the ground. I'd call it a drag race. I've noticed if the male's advances are not received, he stops, returns to a normal stance, and immediately preens his feathers. Soon he's off on another quest.

By mid-morning, many pigeons leave the concrete circle to lounge or rest on lamp posts, trees, buildings, utility lines, or on the ground. In nearby grassy areas, each bird may sit or lean to one side to sunbathe. Female pigeons may preen or rest for a few minutes until an amorous male attempts his "come on."

Visitors and locals offer a variety of grains or junk food to the flock. But pigeons also feed on vegetation, grains, berries, and seeds. Pigeons fly in from several directions to compete. The feathered cluster lures kids to chase them, but pigeons tolerate people's presence.

They are one of the few bird species that can submerge their bills into water to drink without lifting their heads to swallow

Iridescent green and dark fuscia feathers adorn the males more than females. Plumage can vary from black to white, but all have pink legs and feet. Adults sport orange eyes.

When domesticated about six thousand years ago, Rock Pigeons were used as food, to carry messages, or to be revered as symbols of love, faithfulness and dependability. Whether they are called homing, carrier, racing, or war pigeons, they all arose from the wild Rock Pigeon which lived in European and Asian mountains and along coastal cliffs. Distributed throughout the world, pigeons have adapted to city living. City buildings have become their artificial cliffs and ledges and therefore have run "afowl" with people due to their droppings and messy nests. Hence the nickname, "rats with feathers."

For about 800 years, pigeons served as postal carriers. Charlemagne, Charles Darwin, and Queen Victoria raised them due to their beauty. Paul Reuters, founder of Reuters News Agency, used pigeons as carriers of stock market prices. Pigeon racing is still popular – a Chinese enthusiast bought a racing pigeon for $200,000 in 2011. In France and Britain, blood samples from small hospitals are still sent via pigeons to testing facilities as the pigeons are cheaper and faster than a vehicle.

Its importance to humans may be a surprise as Rock Pigeons have been credited with saving thousands of lives!

Before the telegraph, radio or telephone, pigeons were the quickest means of long distance communication.

Genghis Khan and Julius Caesar used them during war. Millions were used as messengers during World Wars I and II, the Korean War, Vietnam War and to detect chemical attacks in the Iraq War. Pigeons were on warships, aircraft, submarines, and even attached to paratroopers.

Many pigeons received medals of honor and awards. Taxonomic specimens of honored birds reside in different museums in Europe and America including a bird named, Cher Ami, French for "dear friend". She earned the French Cross of War for heroism. She served the 77th Infantry from New York in WW 1, behind enemy lines in France.

Cher Ami was the last available pigeon to relay a message for help. When released, the pigeon was shot in the chest and blinded in one eye, but recovered to deliver the message. Cher Ami's leg hung on by a tendon with the attached message. About 200 US Army men were rescued. By the way, the taxidermist realized that Cher Ami was a female, although she was registered in war as a male. Most references today still cite her as a male.

I've only used Cher Ami as one example but one group of carrier pigeons helped in the rescue of 330,000 troops.

I think the pigeons deserve a bow as veteran heroes instead of only considered as "rats with wings."

Note: This article was first published in *Yucatan Today*, Cherie's Bird of the Month-Rock Pigeon, Parts 1 and 2

LORRAINE BAILLIE BOWIE

Gringo Conspiracy

I see myself as honest as most folks. However, when protecting the most senior members of our community from the "Mom and Dad Come Home" Syndrome, I join with my peers to perpetrate a whopper of a deception.

"Rainie, this is Irma, Alice and Albert's daughter in Maine. How are you and Roger?"

"We're all fine Irma," I answered. A sour dry taste of a lie too often told didn't keep me from keeping the necessary secrets.

"How are Mom and Dad? Mom just phoned and said they might not come home this summer, but kind of vague on giving a reason. Is Dad's health worse? I worry about them so far away in Mexico. I know you guys have excellent medical but..."

"Not to worry," I lied without a second thought and gave her the line we all use when adult children of our friends call. "They're fine. I just saw the two of them at a party and your Dad was his old self, cracking jokes and telling stories."

"Rainie please let me know if anything changes. I know they want to stay in Mexico, but we think they're better off close to us."

"Sure will Irma," I said while crossing my fingers behind my back like an eight-year-old telling a fib to a parent.

Alice and Albert, pushing against the high side of eighty, had lived in Merida for twenty-five years, visiting their families for only two months in the summer. This year, Alice wanted to skip the usual drive to Maine as Albert's health was indeed declining.

Albert struggled to swing legs as gnarled as barren twigs over the side of the bed as Alice smoothed the wrinkles from his pillow. "Alice," he said, "If you are okay with driving to Maine, I think we should go."

Alice listened to the familiar old man sounds escape from Albert as he attempted to sit on the side of the bed without assistance. She hesitated as she remembered her upcoming cataract surgery. *Oh well, it can wait.* Running her thin, almost transparent, veined hand over the patchy gray stubble on her husband's head she said, "God Dammit, Albert. We can bloody well do it! "

"Good show my girl. If we don't go, they'll expect the worse. I'm afraid the kids will swoop in on us here in Merida and haul our asses back to Maine."

"Albert, you're still weak from your stroke and Dr. Flores says your heart is struggling. How can we hide that from the kids?"

As Albert looked up to answer her, his eyes met a pixie haircut glistening like newly fallen snow in the sunlight. Glacier blue eyes that still today caused an ache in his soul smiled down at him.

"Just as beautiful as the day we were married," he said as he slipped a hand behind her knee and upwards toward her derrière.

Alice felt a comfortable awe in knowing that the crisscross of wrinkles making a life map across her face was invisible to

Albert. "You old fool," she laughed. "I'm serious. We need to hide your illness from the kids."

"I can sleep in the back of the Blazer while you drive. Then I'll be rested when we get there."

"Yes, and then we can say that you drove most of the way and are tired."

"Alice, I hate for you to have to do all the driving."

"Don't worry Albert; we can stop at night instead of driving straight through like we usually do."

Driving with cataracts ripe for removal was a challenge, but the two decided that sunglasses and a rule of no driving at night would help. Their housekeeper and Albert's home health aide helped Alice pack for the trip. Pablo, who did the heavy work around the house, carried the suitcases to the car. He put down the back seat to make more room for Albert and folded blankets for Albert to lie upon.

Once on the road, Alice learned exactly how much to squint to avoid the pesky halos from the cataracts. Despite the folded blankets, the steel braces in the floor of the backseat pressed against Albert's frail body causing a persistent ache in his lower back. He tried not to complain, but when the ache turned to throbbing, he asked Alice to pull into a Wal-Mart at Veracruz to buy an air mattress. Buying the air mattress was easy, but it turned out Alice and Albert had to inflate it.

After they nearly blew themselves into respiratory failure in the parking lot, a security guard noticed the tailgate was down and approached them to see if they needed assistance. As he peered into the back seat, he saw an old couple as weathered as a forgotten fence with the partially inflated mattress between them. Albert, lying flat on his back, struggled to regain his breath while Alice, sitting cross-legged, coughed into the air valve.

"Do you need help? Can I call anyone for you?"

"Oh no, don't call anyone officer. We're fine, just out of air."

When Alice explained Albert's need for an inflated bed, the guard gathered up the mattress and sprinted to the nearby gas station, returning with a cushy pad filled with air. He situated Albert on his new bed and helped Alice climb out of the back seat. Closing the tailgate, he handed Alice a bag full of gas station goodies and drinks for their trip.

Feeling he should have done more, he waved as Alice pulled out of the parking lot.

"You two have a safe trip now," he called out as he watched the Blazer's turn signal indicate a left turn, as Alice turned right onto the highway.

Years ago Alice and Albert sold the homestead to their oldest daughter, Mattie. A comfortable and cozy guest house on the property was their home for the months of May and June. Mattie, Irma, and their two brothers looked forward to the day when they could convince their parents to live close where they could all take care of them properly.

One evening while Albert slept and Alice watched TV in bed, Mattie burst in with her father's favorite ginger snap cookies. "What are you two doing in bed? It's only 7:30. Is something wrong? Dad looks a little pale. I'll get a doctor's appointment tomorrow."

Dr. Jones was taken aback at Albert's appearance. He'd seen him last year and he seemed okay considering his age. Now he looked gaunt, pale and had an apparent weakness on the left side.

"Albert, when did you have a stroke?"

"Last year, but I didn't tell the kids; they'd make us come back."

"We'll do some tests but I can see right now that you have congestive heart failure, high blood pressure, and probably a low blood count, you're looking pretty pale."

Dr. Jones ordered a barrage of tests and the family made sure Albert showed up for the poking, prodding, and puncturing. After the results had come in, Dr. Jones talked to the two daughters about Albert going into a nursing home. They decided to broach the subject with their parents that very evening. If they needed reinforcements, they could always depend on help from their brothers.

Albert glared at his two daughters, "Listen up girls. I am not going to a home. Your mother and I do fine. It's almost time for us to return to Mexico, so it's out of the question."

"We have everything we need in Merida, so don't worry," said Alice as she moved to stand next to Albert's chair.

The sisters glanced at each other and said no more. Reinforcements were needed and the brothers were called. Later that evening the four children approached their Dad while Alice was in the kitchen giving a great-granddaughter Spanish lessons.

The oldest son, Albert Jr. spoke for the family. "Dad, how can you do this to Mom? Do you have any idea how hard it is for her to take care of you?"

Albert, looking from face to face for a sign of support, found none. "I'll think about it," he said in a voice so small the kids had to strain to hear him.

When Alice finished giving her Spanish lesson, the group approached her before she reached the guest house. "Mom," said Mattie, "can't you see that Dad's health is failing; that he would rather be in a home where he can receive good care?"

Alice said nothing and walked straight to her quarters where Albert had waited up for her. "Albert, do you think you'd be better off in a nursing home?"

Albert, still pondering his children telling him to think of his burden on his wife, said, "I'll go. It might be good to get a little more rehab for my stroke."

Alice still stinging from her children's accusations of her keeping him from care, turned her face to avoid eye contact and said, "Okay, if that's what you really want."

At first Albert pretended to like the nursing home. Alice visited every day; the family came by when they could. Albert remembered the fun the kids had in Mexico when they all came on vacation. It was no longer fun.

One day, at lunch, Alice watched Albert poke holes in his lime Jell-O. "Albert, what's wrong? You're as quiet as a tomb."

"I miss our life in Mexico. I hate to think that we are not going back this year."

As Alice searched for the right words, tears trapped in a crease on her husband's face shocked her to clarity. *My husband deserves the choice to die where he wishes.* "Albert, we can return right now if you like, but I know you are worried about me not taking good care of you."

'"Where did that come from?" he asked.

"Well, the kids thought you wanted to be in the nursing home so I..."

Albert interrupted, "The kids told me I was a burden on you."

"You could never be a burden on me. But, the truth is, it is easier to take care of you in Mexico."

"That's what I thought, but the kids said..."

"Enough about what the children said. They mean well but they are wrong about what we need."

The very next day after Mattie and her husband left for work, Alice loaded up the car, stopped at the gas station to fill up, checked the tires, and got air for the mattress. She drove to the nursing home, walked in with an empty suitcase, packed up Albert's belongings, checked him out against medical advice and headed south.

Alice drove as much as possible each day, pushing her stamina to the limits. From the backseat, Albert sang to keep her awake. Alice didn't mind that the only song he could remember was "You Are My Sunshine."

Once they were back in Merida and Albert had his favorite workers again caring for him, Alice had her cataract surgery. Friends rallied around to help. The net of the conspiracy tightened when their family visited. Everyone reinforced how well Alice and Albert were doing. The quality of the medical and home health care became the main topic of conversation. We all let the family know how they frequently checked on the two, which was the truth and offered to call if anything changed, which was a lie.

On a visit to Merida to check on her parents, Irma pulled me aside. "Rainie, I finally believe that Mom and Dad are well cared for by the expat community. I also see that it is a very close knit group. What I don't understand is why."

"Irma, all immigrants tend to bond together for mutual support."

"But, you are an expat, not an immigrant," Irma said.

"I'm not sure I see the difference. Does it really matter what we are called? We like the term gringo because it gives us a shared identity. The word gringo is, in some areas, a derogatory term, but not in Yucatan. In Yucatan, we gringos insist on using it ourselves which provides the local residents much amusement and causes them to realize that we have a sense of humor and are not above poking fun at ourselves. No matter how integrated most of us are into the Mexican culture, we gringos stay loyal to our class."

Irma raised her left eyebrow to a disapproving arch, "My parents were against a class structure."

"Not social group Irma, but a class made up of others who came to Merida about the same time and had the same renovation ordeals. Your parents are members of the class of 1990 to 2000. We helped each other. The locals didn't relate and the expats who had moved beyond their own renovation horrors tried to appear sympathetic, but their eyes glassed over when we vented. The shared experiences and mutual understanding and support from our class offered a sense of intimacy and trust. In times of high anxiety, we clung together like a litter of pups as we adjusted to a new culture. Now we cling together to support each other through the trials of old age. We will never abandon your parents."

Irma seemed satisfied for the present, but because she still suffered from the "Mom and Dad Come Home" Syndrome, I held back an important fact:

We remain loyal to our class until the end. We'll even conspire to protect each other's right to draw our last breath here.

Retirees who decide to live and die here have the respect of their peers.

"Don't call my kids."

"I never will. Promise not to call mine?"

CHERIE PITTILLO

Broken Rainbow

Purple Gallinule

Dawn awakes
Shadows sleep
Rain drips

Sun rises
Rainbow breaks
Color cascades

Wind whispers
Faith leaps
Joy uplifts

Sun glows
Leaves applaud
Standing ovation

First published in The Yucatan Times, Backyard Birding in Merida, Yucatan and Beyond.

CHERIE PITTILLO

Chainsaws and Homeless

When I heard the roar of a chainsaw, my heart sank. I ran to our parking lot in our block…and stopped. And stared in disbelief. I was too late.

A tree was gone. Tears welled up. I ran back to my home, grabbed my camera and returned to see yet another tree cut down.

I had photographed those trees for more than two years. Almost every time I went in or out of this lot for five years, I looked at those trees, the headless palm tree and a dead snag.

Although I may sound like a "tree hugger," I'm not. Keep reading.

The one Royal Palm served as a beacon to attract birds to nest or roost in its tree cavities carved out by woodpeckers. One of the woodpecker-made holes attracted a pair of Red-lored Parrots in 2010. Both adults took turns reshaping the entry and pulling out tree tissue until a pair of White-fronted Parrots claimed it on Feb. 18, 2011. I never saw the Red-lored Parrots again after their lengthy efforts to make a nest for several months.

(Yes, at least three species of parrots live in Merida.)

In 2012, a Golden-fronted Woodpecker chipped and chunked out a new nesting cavity mouthful by mouthful below where the White-fronted Parrots arrived to nest.

If two nesting sites in this palm for two species weren't enough, enter the Great Kiskadee pair to adorn the leafless top with their nest.

Life became tricky for the parrots. It seemed the male parrot would distract the territorial kiskadee to chase it to give the female time to sneak into the nest hole.

Meanwhile the woodpecker could swoop into its nest unscathed from the kiskadees, but it would stick its head out of its nest to check for the pesky neighbors before it departed. Three different species tried to nest within 15 feet of each other.

Both the kiskadees and woodpeckers raised their broods. The parrots experimented about housekeeping especially since each time they tried to enter their nest, they were met with a tyrant flycatcher (kiskadee) chasing the bejesus out of them. Plus parrots can work on their nest for several seasons before the nest is finalized. However, the male Golden-fronted Woodpecker continued to use its former nest as a "man cave" until Feb. 5, 2013.

Both the kiskadees and White-fronted Parrots have been active at their nest sites. Recently two pairs of parrots crashed through limbs, chased each other, and screaming bloody murder...or so it sounded to me. This was the most intense, loudest aggression I've witnessed between two pairs. Why? Competition for that former tree cavity was that keen.

That is the crux of why I'm upset.

How many available nesting locations are here in Centro? No one knows.

Just think how long it took the Golden-fronted Woodpecker to whittle out a place to roost or nest. Other birds, snakes, lizards, and small mammals can use these abandoned tree cavities for roosting or raising young. Thank goodness the woodpecker got things started. Bit by bit by tiny bit. Day after day of carving. How much wood can a woodpecker's mouth hold and then release out of its mouth? Spit happens. It's a time-consuming, slow task.

Would it have made any difference to the owner of that property whether or not that tree provided nest sites or that three active nests existed? I don't know.

Does it matter that the nearby snag was also cut down? Yes, I know it was dead. I would call it "sculptural." Others would say "ugly." But this old, dead tree gave the woodpeckers a place to mate several times close to their nest. Also it provided a respite from the nest sculpting and served as the local grocery store filled with beetles and other insects for both parents and their young. In addition, the parent birds would also store food in this "pantry."

Orioles, pygmy-owls, and grackles used it as a perch or lookout while ground-doves found it ideal for brief hook-ups with responsive females. Even the male parrot stood guard while the female worked the nest. Sometimes both parrots preened each other on it. That action helps maintain social bonding while it keeps skin and feathers in good condition.

Maybe all I can do is share the experience and explain the importance to save those nesting places as long as the host tree wouldn't endanger people or property if it fell. I don't think the snag would have done any damage; the palm hasn't appeared to move for five years.

Finally I realize part of my emotion is thinking about how many hours at dawn and evening I spent to photograph and observe these birds for over two years. Sometimes I hid behind cars in the parking lot or sat in the car so I wouldn't disturb any of the birds. I've sweated through many hours patiently waiting for the birds to arrive. But now, all of my data seems naught. I hoped for parrot chicks this year. Then I could share this story of three different species inhabiting this columnar condo. I felt protective about that tree because I knew the "inside" story. People who saw me in the parking lot asked what I was doing. No one admitted they had seen any birds or their nests until I showed them.

As I write this, the parrots just flew overhead squawking and didn't stop for their ritual evening concert. By the way, they didn't return the next morning, but the woodpecker continues to search for its hideaway.

My heart still hurts.

First published in The Yucatan Times, Backyard Birding in Merida, Yucatan and Beyond.

MARYETTA ACKENBOM

Owlet

Ferruginous Pygmy-Owl, Glaucidium brasilianum. Cherie, her husband Greenwood, and I rescued this precious four-inch tall fledgling from my backyard, where it was crouched in a corner by the back door, facing down my two terriers and other birds. We released it in a safer area behind Cherie's house.

I stretched my wings and peeked over the edge of the nest cavity. Could I climb out? My sister shrieked and I tumbled back. Maybe not today.

But I knew I was ready. I just knew it! I had all my feathers. Mom and Dad had been stuffing both of us with fat grubs and bits of mice and lizards. I was ready to go.

Bit by bit I clawed my way to the edge of the nest hole. Holding on, trying to balance. Sister shrieked again, warning me, calling Mom and Dad. I wobbled, and fell out.

I waved my wings as hard as I could, but I was still falling. A soft landing, into a pile of leaves. The wings did help. But I couldn't stay here.

I started flapping those wings again. They helped me take long leaps, almost airborne.

I heard another shriek—not my people, this time. Other birds. After me! I flew-hopped as fast as I could, hunting a place to hide.

Oops—no, don't want to go there—lots of water, and I sure couldn't swim. Hop. Fly. Hop. Ah, a protected corner. I backed in and stared around, rested a bit, but still scared.

I heard a roar, then a yip. A monster looked down at me, then backed away. Hey, that was pretty good—guess I scared it! That's what owls are supposed to do. That's why we have bright yellow eyes and a swiveling neck.

A shadow fell on me and I looked up into the eyes of an even larger monster. It looked at me. I glared back. It disappeared. Good!

But it came back, and reached behind me—and lifted me! I squirmed and tried to claw and bite but it held me tight.

Then it placed me in a cave. It was almost dark so I was calmer. But every so often, the cave moved. I kept still. It seemed like forever. Several times the mouth of the cave opened a crack and I glimpsed the great monster peeking in at me. I glared at it and it went away.

Then the whole cage moved, and kept moving. I felt a vibration that seemed like it would never stop. Hours or days later, my cave was moved again. The whole mouth of it opened and the cave turned. I didn't want to leave it—I was terrified!

But after a few minutes, the cave turned more, and I couldn't hold on. I slid out.

Now wings, do your stuff!

They did. I didn't fly very far, but I felt like my wings were much stronger, and I landed in a tree. Not where my nest was, but a new tree, and I could move from branch to branch, and even to other trees. I sensed worms and small animals which I knew I could catch and eat.

And other birds—not my kind—which mobbed me, trying to chase me away.

But I was good at hiding by now. I found a place among the limbs where I rested, and then started out again into this great, grand world.

GWEN LANE

Scrambled Breakfast

It takes more than some college level Spanish classes to fully understand the fast talk and colloquialisms of native speakers. The optimist within me decided my tourist Spanish always got me by before and my language skills good enough to move to the Yucatan. But nothing prepares one for living in a different country with a different language day to day to day. On demanding days my head spun around correct verb usage, (if I could figure out the verb at all) difficulties in finding just the right English word to translate, confusion and frustration.

Our Spanish language life line, my husband, had unfinished business north of the border during this time. He thought he had good Spanish skills until dealing with new words for household items and construction, plumbing, electrical, lawyers, doctors and banks. I muddled through the daily business alone and maintained my sanity while adjusting to new happenings and our four year old triplets commencing their first year of kindergarten. Their teacher spoke English, although no better than my Spanish.

Ten weeks after the start of school, in conjunction with lessons on good health, hygiene and manners, the school invited the moms to a breakfast and show. Fortunately, their teacher realized my situation and explained to me the day before the importance of having someone there for each child. I planned on attending alone because the invitation said "Mom's breakfast". I breathed a sigh of relief knowing Papa had returned two days before and brought Grandma with him.

I have no idea where I got my missed communications. It couldn't have anything to do with my level of understanding the notes sent home. I'm sure the root of the problem lies with the subtleness of the language and people.

For example, on the third day of school the children came home with a notebook with lines drawn in ink by the teacher across the top. The next day she wrote a note in the book about the importance of parent participation in helping children learn. I asked someone at the hotel where we stayed while our house remodel finished, what the children needed to do in the books. The teacher had not given me any instruction and the children didn't know. The hotel worker had children and told me the teacher wanted them to draw the shapes.

The same week a note came home that asked parents to purchase a mesh carry bag for each child. It stated they could be bought at the usual places.

When I told the teacher I didn't know the usual places, she tried to be helpful.

"Well, I think there is one on 65 downtown between 54 and 56, no on 63 across from the big red pharmacy building. Or is it between 56 and 58?"

She must have noticed the dazed and confused look on my

face and glazed eyes. I asked her to repeat the directions while I rubbed my temples and wondered if I should try to follow her directions with three small ones in tow or venture solo.

I've learned that this is Yucatan directions, using landmarks and incorrect street numbers. Over the years I have increasingly used this form of direction since the street numbering is difficult to follow in Merida. It seems to be a collection of *colonias*, small neighborhoods that over the years have merged into the big city but kept their neighborhood numbering. This leads to confusion sometimes when one side of the street is one number and the other side a different number and in different *colonia*.

Their teacher suggested she had to go downtown and would pick three bags up for me. I could pay her later.

But, for today the children's usual play area had turned into a dining room and stage. Small flower arrangements and napkin holders with images of cuddly animals adorned the tables, and pictures of fruits, vegetables, and children using good hygiene habits. A teacher called each child from their classroom and they came and greeted each one of us at the door wearing a chef hat and apron with purple grapes and green vines painted on them. We followed each one to a table. Somewhere on that walk my smile turned shaky and my heart sank as I realized that the children served us breakfast. Of course, what was I thinking? How would the moms serving the kids be different from any other day?

Do I confess to the teacher and tell her that I withheld breakfast from my children and they're running on empty? What kind of mother does that? At least, I got an adult here for each child to serve.

Each child handed their guest a menu and program, walked over to the serving table and brought us juice and a small plate with fruit and a muffin, and asked if we wanted scrambled eggs or *chilaquiles,* basically scrambled eggs with crisp tortillas and a red or green sauce.

I shyly walked over to the teacher and struggled to find the right words to explain my misunderstanding of this whole breakfast thing. "*No te preocupas*", don't worry, she told me. I had learned that phrase fast when the teacher repeated and repeated and repeated it the first and second days of school while she gently pushed me out of the classroom as tears ran down the faces of all four of us.

She assured me they had enough food and would offer them some. It still troubled me and every time one of my children passed I offered some of what ever filled my plate. None of them took my offers of food.

First the three year olds toddled onto stage. They wiggled and stomped their way through a song with helpful reminders and hints from their teachers on the sidelines. One youngster, unable to stay still and bouncing from foot to foot abruptly ran from the stage. His chef hat with a picture of a pineapple fell to the floor. His pants hovered around his ankles as he waddled the rest of the way to the bathroom. We always laughed at our house too when our children did not want to stop playing and that happened.

The four year olds bodies' swayed constantly in motion with grand gestures, waved arms and lifted feet. I felt warmth and love radiating throughout and my eyes grew heavy with moisture as I watched my little ones, in their first theatrical debut. They sang with light hearts and glowing smiles. No one cared if they missed a cue or foot stomp.

The movements and coordination of the five years olds appeared better than the two younger groups and they relied less on their teacher's prompts.

For the finale, all the groups sang together about eating healthy foods and exercise.

After the show we could leave the children till the end of school or take them with us. Even though my kindergarten blues had quieted, I still missed the morning company of my children and I eagerly took them home, and unscrambled breakfast.

Moments weave the tapestry of our lives. Today mine added a sparkling strand for each heart that was there for the love of a child, a strand for each golden voice that sang to me. Strands of silver for smiles and laughter that filled the air and a multi colored ribbon that ties together my scrambled breakfast that added a magnificent unique piece to the tapestry of my life.

LORNA GAIL DALLIN

An Embarrassing Moment...

When asked recently to recount a story of embarrassment, personal or otherwise, which has occurred in my ex-pat life in Mexico; I confess I was stumped.

Stories of mangled Spanish abound but what about an embarrassing moment perhaps of a cultural nature? And what is embarrassing anyway. To me it is a time when I say to myself, "you should have known better" or "you have inadvertently made someone else uncomfortable". Embarrassment comes of feeling inadequate.

It was my first Christmas living in Mexico when I made one of The Great Errors: I *assumed*. I assumed that everyone in Mexico celebrated Christmas just the way I celebrated it. I assumed and thereby, as the old saw goes: "ASSUME made an ASS out of U and ME." That ASS lead me to embarr-ass.

Could I have been completely unaware of the Mexican celebration of the Eve of Christmas, the celebration at the midnight hour at which time Christ is born and then dinner is served? Who knew? I had invited folks to a Christmas Eve soiree at my casa, anyone I had met over the past few months of living on Isla Mujeres, gringos and Mexican friends. The invite was for 7.00 pm or so – when there is still some daylight – I thought. I had no electricity at my little palapa by the sea. Gas lamps and candles were going to be light enough.

Comes the appointed hour; I am sitting by the door, ready to light the candles the minute people start arriving. I am still sitting, waiting, at 9.00 pm. At 10.00, my visiting friend goes to bed and I begin to close up shop. Gas lamps out, I think I will take a walk around my palapa and nurse my outrage and hurt feelings. I am just about to crawl into my hammock at about 11.00 when people start showing up. I fumble around, get the gas lamps back on and hiss at my friend to get up and light the candles. As we get back into the celebration mode, I keep apologizing for not being "ready". No one seems to mind, not a word about them being late. The savvy gringos knew enough to not come early. The Mexicans expected to be there at midnight.

The actual embarrassment came later when I saw how stupid I had been in making my assumptions about how we celebrate Christmas. My penchant for "my way or no way" was going to have to be subsumed, swallowed, negotiated, if I was not to embarrass myself again and again in this Mexican landscape in which I had chosen to live.

Grace Note: When I took that walk around my palapa before the guests arrived, carrying a small flashlight; I came to the east side of the house looking out to sea. In the utter darkness of my location, the stars were myriad. The vastness of the firmament quite struck me, enough to make me gasp at the overwhelming spectacle of it. There was an actual weight to seeing that many stars. My puny flashlight stayed by my side and I walked out into the natural setting of my home and gaped at the ceiling provided me: The stars of a Christmas Eve in Mexico.

MARYETTA ACKENBOM

The Neophyte Birdwatcher

There, in that tree, that must be a Clay-colored Thrush! Just like Cherie described it. And it's in the book. And its song is so similar to the recording.

I acquired the book several years ago, when I realized that the birds I was hearing were quite different from those in my native Oklahoma. I knew robins and Blue Jays and mockingbirds and crows. My mother would spot them first and point them out to me—sometimes I'd see them, often I couldn't.

Same here in Merida. Sometimes I can see that Clay-colored Thrush, often I can't. Cherie says, "You need binoculars."

I have a beautiful pair of binoculars. They don't work fast enough for me, though, and they won't penetrate leaves or block out the obstructing sun.

My birdwatching was truly hit-or-miss, mostly miss, until I found Cherie Pittillo in my Merida Writers' Group. Cherie was putting together a series of stories about her encounters with wild animals, mostly in Africa. Then Cherie got a new camera, and after a trial period, she began a famous series of bird articles in publications about Yucatan. Cherie's pictures were so good that she has been invited on several excursions of professional photographers. Some of her best articles are included here, in *Uniquely Yucatan*.

So I began to try to identify the birds I saw or heard in and around my backyard. First was the hummingbird, cinnamon-colored, which was entranced by the flower spikes on my aloe vera plantings. I saw the bird, Cherie wrote about it, and lo! I had its name.

Warblers began to plague me, because I could never find them among the greenery. I could catch glimpses, but I was never sure the bird I saw was the one singing. Then there was the Clay-colored Thrush. I got you down, sweetie! What a pretty song.

Another songster still hides from me. I've concocted a libretto to its tune, something like "Her hair is prettee." I'm waiting for Cherie to find that one for me.

I watched parrots—how did I know there was more than one kind?—when they flew over the neighborhood and occasionally rested atop my neighbor's tree. Now I know that there are different ones, sometimes fighting their cousins for territory.

Grackles, I thought I knew. No, there are several different species of large black birds, and I've never gotten close enough to identify the ani and the blackbird.

Pigeons. Not just pigeons, *Rock* Pigeons. They sit atop the water tank on my roof, looking entirely innocent of their long, fabulous history as messengers.

White-winged Doves are everywhere during their breeding season, and very prolific. I can't vouch for their intelligence. They tend to fly into walls, with fatal results. It's good they're prolific.

And the little Ruddy Ground-Doves, always seen in pairs or small groups, almost always on the ground. They also must be prolific.

I will not forget the marvelous picture of the Purple Gallinule, Cherie's pride. Someday, perhaps, I will witness such a sight.

I never knew there were so many lovely birds! Thank you, Cherie, for enhancing the beauty of my garden.

CHERIE PITTILLO

A Cat Burglar from the Get Go? No, a Gecko!

"Someone tried to break into our rental house. We heard someone scratching on the window screen," exclaimed my visiting friends from New Jersey.

I couldn't believe my friends. Merida is the city of peace, of safety, not crime.

The parents had gathered up their two kids, blocked their bedroom door, and waited with kitchen knives for the burglar to appear. He or she or it never did.

I said, "Did you hear anything else?"

"No, only the loud scratching on the screen."

"Aha," I replied. "You didn't have a burglar. That noisemaker is the denizen of the dark, a denizen of the den, bedroom, kitchen, bath, and living room. What you heard was the loud call of a gecko!"

"We didn't know lizards had voices!"

"I know it seems strange, but geckos here emit a raspy, scratchy-type sound or a chirpy, froggy-like call. I remember when we first arrived in our Merida home, we heard an unknown sound. We walked into our bathroom and turned on a light. On the concrete ceiling were two dark-eyed, tan lizards that looked attached to it. We named the three inch one, Greg Gecko, and the two inch one, Meg. They ran upside down along the ceiling, down part of the wall, and then hid behind a light fixture.

"Not only can they defy gravity by running upside down, they seem to adhere to glass. Their toe pad soles consist of millions of hair-like structures that can wedge into the glass or ceiling surfaces. Now scientists have learned these hairs become stickier with humidity. Merida easily provides humidity for them!

"You don't need to worry about them, because they are harmless to us. These night-time critters feed on mosquitoes and other insects. Since they climb walls and ceilings, sometimes you may see their tiny whitish and brown/black turds on chair cushions. People may think a mouse dropped by, but nope, it's the common house gecko."

"Thanks for letting us know. We'll sleep well tonight."

GWEN LANE

The Wandering Iguanas

As I wandered through my house as I do most days because my house is the perfect size for a daily wander, I discovered, to my great surprise, that a baby iguana had wandered into my upstairs open roofed tub.

I sat on the stair outside the tub where I could watch and talk to my new little friend. Although it is called a Black Iguana, the head and upper body looked green to me. I learned later that the two most common species of iguanas in the Yucatan start out green. The brown tail looked as long as the body. It stuck out its tongue and crawled around the slick concrete, unable to climb the one step to freedom.

Perhaps it sunned in my tub by choice; I liked to use it and maybe iguanas did too. The slow pace and methodical way the iguanas merge with their surroundings is Zen-like to watch; there's no other moment but now and communion with the sun and silent search for warmth and food.

I've held large captive iguanas before but prefer to look at reptiles and did not care to handle this one. I wonder what the iguanas think about while sunning themselves. Could it be anything like what some humans think while sunbathing? "Hey, Iggy, check out those stripes on the new girl next door."

Perhaps they ponder in deep hypnotic thought about their ancestry and evolution. Or maybe they just want to get warm. These cold-blooded animals use sun and shade to regulate their body temperature. Different types of iguanas wander around the world including Mexico, Central America, Brazil and the Caribbean Islands.

Suddenly it puffed out and I thought it showed a red throat. I ran downstairs, quick feet returned me with the camera. I had hoped the iguana had not left while I tarried. This playful youngster was still eager to pose. I snapped away. After a while I questioned why it had not grown bored with my company and scurried away.

While descending the stairs again to solicit assistance from Hubby, I decided to email a few pics to my zoologist, naturalist, friend, Cherie for her advice. She helped to determine the correct species of reptile and informed me it is difficult to tell the males from the females at this stage.

Geckos and other small reptiles are permitted in our home for their insect eating instincts. We have several that live in the small garden outside of our kitchen and shelter themselves in the cupboard. We all know they live there, yet they still manage to startle sometimes when caught scurrying across the back wall.

We appreciate our cats' hunting abilities for eliminating cockroaches and mice and discourage her instincts for chasing the birds and bothering the lizards, but still we see many lizards without tails. Most lizards and iguanas can detach a part of their tail to ensure escape from a predator. The tail soon heals but rarely reaches its previous size, usually half of their body length.

THE WANDERING IGUANAS

I warn my guests that their bed and bath accommodations include a couple of small resident lizards. They sneak behind the bathroom mirror and I've seen them come and go through cracks in the screen but they never bother anyone.

With memories still fresh of Hubby's hunt and successful capture and release of not one, but two wayward baby iguanas wandering the sidewalk in front of our house, he joined my quest to free another one. Perhaps this is one of the iguanas he rescued from possible road kill a few weeks ago with the help of our friend, Atah. His agility and quick feet helped immensely to apprehend the wandering iguanas. Or perhaps this is another similar looking, adventuresome, clumsy baby iguana.

The men paraded through the living and dining rooms that afternoon like triumphant warriors returned from a hunt. One holding the end of the long handle of the swimming pool net and one keeping the two iguanas contained in it. As they passed they stopped briefly in the kitchen to a round of applause, and proudly held up and showed us their prize.

They released them high on the wall in our backyard where the small reptiles found entrances to what I refer to as, their hidden haciendas, (small openings between rocks and brick walls where the iguanas live) behind the climbing flowers. The Black Iguana is primarily herbivorous; it likes to eat fruits, leaves and flowers, but it also eats eggs and baby birds.

We planted the climbing *copa de oro,* cup of gold, to make a garden in front of their hidden hideouts.

No damage occurred to this wandering one from a fall of fifteen feet, off a support beam into the tub below. Iguanas can survive falls from the height of 40 feet without injuries.

"He can't get out from here, it's too slick. I'll be back in a minute." Hubby left to gather equipment for his plan.

Hubby thought himself an iguana catcher after his capture

and release of those two iguanas back into their more natural and safe habitat. He again swung the long handled swimming pool net in an attempt to capture our friend and return it safely to its home; although as he had previously learned, iguanas are skilled at alluding capture.

One glimpse as he entered the tub and the iguana sensed entrapment, not help, and our visitor ran directly to his only escape, the drain. I never imagined it would be able to squeeze down the pipes or I would have plugged it before the chase.

Hubby and I looked at each other with disbelief and shock. We came to a dead stop and stared at each other with gaping mouths and wide eyes that said, "Did you see that?" thinking we had sent him to a watery grave.

I remembered my last experience with a wandering iguana and a drain. We had to remove a dead one blocking an outside rain drain so water would not overflow the roof and fall into the house.

"Now look what you've done." In typical marriage fashion, he blamed me that the iguana had chosen a watery death instead of jumping into the net for a ride home to show its appreciation for the help.

"Don't blame me," I countered. "It trusted me and we got along fine till your bright idea to bring that net up here. It posed and let me shoot photos."

An unnatural quiet filled the air, a moment of silent remembrance. "I guess we'll wait and see what happens." I climbed out of the tub, shaking my head.

Fifteen minutes later I quietly entered the bathroom and peered into the tub. A sigh of relief escaped my lips when I realized we had not killed it yet. It had returned from the drain and we would not have to figure out how to remove another one from the pipes. The second it saw me, it ran down the drain again to save its life, or so it thought.

I wouldn't have been so concerned if I had known that most species of iguanas are excellent swimmers and can spend up to twenty-eight minutes under the water without returning to the surface for air.

The same scenario played out again half hour later.

Back downstairs I questioned hubby, "We need plan B, any ideas?"

"Yes. Glad you asked." Obviously, he had already been devising another plan.

"It needs some kind of ladder or steps to bypass the slick wall of the tub. I'll see what I can find to help."

Ten minutes later he announced he had placed a stepping stone, against the wall of the tub that the iguana can get traction on.

We haven't had another animal wander into the tub. We hope our young friend used the emergency steps and stayed close by living a healthy and long, twenty-year average iguana lifespan, in the wild.

GWEN LANE

State of Yucaland

I dreamed one night of a Yucatan,
Where waters run sweet, next to white sands.
Jaguars roar and roam all night,
Bats fly high in search of food till light.
As I wonder in this state of Yucatan,
Not sure if it's a state of mind or land.
The nights linger hot and the days burn long,
Whispering winds play a tranquil song.
Here within my yuca mind,
I find my place in yuca time.
And once upon a yuca time,
When giants and centaurs filled my mind;
An enormous rock hit yuca land and thus began the Yucatan.
Perhaps some new species came from that steamy crater,
To begin things new again, grander and much greater.
My mind drifts to a time in Yucatan,
When wondrous pyramids filled the land.
Snakes and reptiles climbed around,
Trees and vegetation ruled the ground.

UNIQUELY YUCATAN

I love my state of Yucatan,
Unicorns and dragons rule the land.
Bright blossoms full of browsing bees,
Where my mind runs wild and my thoughts are free.
On this piece of land called Yucatan,
Grow coconuts and bananas, picked by hand.
Mangos, peppers, papayas and limes,
Have survived throughout the times.
Always in my yuca mind,
Never know what I might find.
The plants and animals in yuca earth,
Bring to my heart and soul a yuca mirth.
Coyotes and foxes howl at night,
Fearless felines prowl, out of sight.
I love the yuca sands of Yucatan,
Where I will make my final stand.
Caves, cenotes, beaches, lagoons,
Mangroves, marines and the dunes.
Iguanas, geckos, toads and lizards galore,
Seek the sun, from the yuca lands to the yuca shores.
In my yuca state where heaven meets the sky,
I sit upon my yuca cloud and watch the birds go by.
Woodpeckers, flycatchers and hummingbirds,
Toucans and tanagers, too beautiful for words.
Great ocean waves splash and spill beneath my yuca land,
On my paradise island, waits a handsome yuca merman.
Smiling silence in my yuca thoughts,
Reveal peace and love that can't be bought.
Always in my mind, sometimes on the land
Now I made my yuca stand in my state of Yucatan.

About the Authors

Maryetta Ackenbom: Maryetta graduated from a career with the U.S. Foreign Service and has chosen to live in Merida permanently. She has been writing short stories for twenty years or so, and has published a number of them with online magazines. Her first novel, *Georgia's Hope*, was published last year, and she's now working on the sequel.

Lorraine Baillie Bowie PhD: Rainie is a noted sex and relationship expert who retired to Merida with her husband Roger 11 years ago. In addition to her fascination with the geckos living behind the pictures on the wall of her library, she has published two self-help books, *Win at Love* and *The Science of Finding Love That Lasts*. Her short stories about the human condition, especially about living in the Yucatan, are published in two anthologies. Living 'round the corner from the legendary English Library provides Rainie with a never-ending parade of diverse characters with outrageous-but-true-stories that have to be fictionalized to be believed.

Lorna-Gail Dallin: Lorna-Gail has been writing all her life and not just since she "retired". Through her several careers she has written advertising copy, promotional copy, exhortation copy, minutes of meetings, annual reports, mission statements, grants, proposals, newsletters, love letters and letters home. These days she likes writing about what is going on around her and within her. There seems to be enough to keep her in material for stories and essays.

Theresa Diaz Gray: Theresa is a published author and blogger who has lived in Mérida since 2004. A confirmed, do it yourselfer, she likes to undertake interesting projects and write about them. Having survived breast cancer, she is focused in living in the present and seizing all the opportunities that life offers.

Gwen Lane: Gwen finds fun penning her adventures as a mother raising triplets and other humorous observations and experiences. One day, as the flow of time and energy permit, she will compile her Triplet Tales into a captivating and clever publication.

Cherie Pittillo: Whether flying in a microlight over Africa, hanging from a helicopter to photograph nature, tickling a 350-pound gorilla, or dodging a charging rhinoceros, Cherie Pittillo owes her destiny to her birth as the first baby born at the hospital at Bat Cave, North Carolina. She is a writer, award-winning photographer, and zoologist with an MS in Biology. Her publications vary from BBC Books' *Incredible Journeys* to the African edition of *Reader's Digest*. As a columnist, Pittillo continues to write "Backyard Birding in Merida, Yucatan and Beyond" for *The Yucatan Times*.

Made in the USA
Charleston, SC
14 January 2016